"If your life is ever going to get better, you'll have to take chances."

—Dr. David Viscott

Risking is a book about taking chances: about freeing yourself so you can recognize and take *your* chances for love, power, and self-esteem. In *Risking,* Dr. Viscott explains step-by-step how to face the risks which will help you reach your dreams. Some of his guidelines:

HAVE A GOAL:
"A risk taken without a clear purpose is in trouble from the start."

ASK QUESTIONS:
"If you are going to take a risk unnecessarily, you are most likely to do so because you were afraid to ask questions. It's better to appear stupid than to make a big mistake."

KNOW THE LOSS INVOLVED:
"If you don't expect the loss, you don't understand the risk."

TAKE YOUR OWN RISKS:
"Whenever you allow someone to take your risks for you, you are putting your fate into the hands of someone who cannot take your interest to heart the way you would.

READ *RISKING*. IT'S A CHANCE YOU OUGHT TO TAKE.

Books by David Viscott, M.D.

How to Live with Another Person
The Language of Feelings
Risking
The Viscott Method: A Revolutionary Program
    for Self-Analysis and Self-Understanding

Published by POCKET BOOKS

RISKING

BY
DAVID VISCOTT, M.D.

PUBLISHED BY POCKET BOOKS NEW YORK

POCKET BOOKS, a division of Simon & Schuster, Inc.
1230 Avenue of the Americas, New York, N.Y. 10020

Published by arrangement with Simon & Schuster, Inc.
Library of Congress Catalog Card Number: 77-21779

ISBN: 0-671-62690-6

First Pocket Books printing May, 1979

16   15   14   13   12   11   10   9

POCKET and colophon are registered trademarks
of Simon & Schuster, Inc.

Printed in the U.S.A.

*For Teddy
and Judy Kaplan*

Contents

Security is mostly a superstition. It does not exist in nature, nor do the children of men as a whole experience it. Avoiding danger is no safer in the long run than outright exposure. Life is either a daring adventure or nothing.

—HELEN KELLER

RISKING

Introduction

If your life is ever going to get better, you'll have to take risks. There is simply no way you can grow without taking chances.

It is surprising how little most people know about taking risks. Often people become inhibited by fear at the very moment they must commit themselves to action. At the first sign of a reversal they doubt themselves, hesitate and, fearing that the situation is about to fall apart, retreat untested, convinced that they were in over their heads, thankful just to escape. They do not understand that to risk is to exceed one's usual limits in reaching for any goal, and that uncertainty and danger are simply part of the process.

This book is a guide to help you understand exactly what happens whenever you risk. It will not only indicate the steps involved in successful risking, but will also explain the troublesome feelings that accompany taking a chance, feelings that can build within you and spoil your success even when you are doing everything else correctly. It will tell you where these feelings come from and how to master them. This book will also show where the potential dangers lie in the most common risking situations and how to manage them to minimize your possible losses and increase your gains.

Don't be put off by the tone of this book. It's meant to be real, not clever or seductive. If you're going to learn about taking a risk, you don't want to be misled to believe it's easy. Putting your excuses for not risking aside, there's a lot you're now not getting and still need but are afraid to reach for, so you already know how difficult it is to take a risk. The questions that are going to be discussed here are real and important. They are going to be discussed straightforwardly and in a way that you can directly apply to your life right now.

This book would be dishonest if it tried to encourage you to take a risk you were unprepared for or really didn't need. It is still not possible for some people to take a risk until they know they will lose more by not risking. Unfortunately when a situation is allowed to go that far, a person's strength, resources, and confidence are often so eroded that the chances of success are greatly reduced.

This book will help you find courage to risk through understanding the nature of risking in general and your own risk in particular. It will help you take strength from guidelines that you can believe in, that are not frivolous, that offer you perspective to put the moment of risk in its proper place. You won't have to wait for circumstances to deteriorate to force you to act. The purpose of this book is to help you find courage—real courage, not just something made up—not through any gimmicks or coercion but through examining the truth, evaluating your particular needs, recognizing your own self-worth, accepting that you deserve the best you can make for yourself and assuming your responsibility to act.

The greatest courage comes from the highest conviction. No amount of technique alone will make it possible for you to take risks unless you recognize a need to change and believe in your objectives. This guide will sort out some of the confusion, ambivalence, guilt and dishonesty that everyone experiences in risking and help you discover a goal that is right for you. Its purpose is to help you create a life worth living and to find the courage from within to risk pursuing your dream and making it real.

When you have an objective worth risking for, your actions become purposeful and your life begins to make sense, and then no risk can hold you back.

1

Taking Chances

This is a book about risking, about taking a chance. It's a book about doing it, about putting your cards on the table, declaring yourself, picking the right time and going for broke.

In other words, this is a book about life.

Risking! The sound of the word alone is enough to make you pause.

To risk is to loosen your grip on the known and the certain and to reach for something you are not entirely sure of but you believe is better than what you now have, or is at least necessary to survive.

Taking a risk is central to everything worthwhile in life. Without taking a risk, no one finds true love, no one develops real power and no one gains prestige.

Everything you really want in life involves taking a risk.

TAKING A LEAP

You cannot grow without taking a risk, a chance. At each stage in our growth we become a little stronger, a bit more self-confident. Although we seem to grow by steps, each phase of growth is not really accomplished by a step, but by a leap. That is precisely why risking is so fearful and why growing is so painful. Like all risks, growing requires giving something up without knowing for certain if the next step will be any better. If growth were stepwise, logical and predictable, there would be much less risk involved, and more people would find success and happiness in life.

When a person grows he gives up an old way of seeing himself. Part of the pain of growing comes from realizing you have been dishonest with yourself, and this discomfort motivates people to change. It always takes a leap to give up what is false, but once you become aware that you have been fooling yourself you cannot help being much more honest. To maintain the old self-deception once you become aware makes your life less real and drains your energy.

Like growing, risking is concerned with giving up false beliefs, compromised allegiances, misdirected investments, superficial attachments and destructive habits.

But false beliefs are often supported by good faith. When a person loses faith in a long-held belief he feels empty and needs something new to believe in. ·

Allegiances are often made in the belief that there is safety in numbers and in the hope that one's loyalty will be returned when the need arises. People who shed allegiances made out of fear—be they to an institution, a profession, a union or a political party—quickly seek out new allies to take the place of old ones.

Bad investments cannot be written off without pain. An investment of friendship or love is no less painful to lose than one of money, time or energy. It is difficult but necessary to admit that your efforts, resources and feelings were misplaced.

Attachments held out of fear do not really serve us. Yet many people yearn for their parents to change and long to be understood, loved, respected, cared for or accepted. They need to believe their parents have the capacity to give even when everything they know suggests they never could or will.

We hold on to bad habits because we are not really committed to grow and we need an excuse for our failures. We keep our bad habits because we do not really love ourselves.

Clinging rigidly to a false belief impedes growth. For example, continuing to believe your mother really meant well when she hurt you stifles you with anger you feel too guilty to vent. Believing that you could be a brilliant student if you really tried makes you avoid working up to your potential. You never succeed and so doubt yourself and the value of trying. False beliefs stand between you and reality. Until you yield to the truth, you can never succeed as yourself.

The threat of losing the false security of old beliefs undermines your ability to risk. Even a trivial risk can evoke great fear when it questions a cherished belief. For example, the man who cannot risk accepting a promotion because he fears testing his worth may sabotage his own progress, or the child who fears his parents do not love him may avoid questioning the truth by never disobeying. When your viewpoint is threatened your entire world feels insecure. No one likes to admit the problem is *him!*

THE LOSS BEHIND EACH RISK

In every risk there is some unavoidable loss, something that has to be given up to move ahead. Nothing overwhelms a person taking a chance like the unexpected discovery of a loss he has not seen before. Even if you cannot define the specific loss, any potential loss affects you. In fact, the vague fear that you are going to lose *something* may have a greater inhibiting effect than knowing exactly what that something is. At least if you knew what you feared losing, you would be prepared to protect yourself. When an unexpected fear catches you by surprise, you begin to doubt your judgment and your plans. Knowing you are going to lose something helps, and knowing what that something is helps more.

Many people are terrified by any possible loss and try to avoid all risks. They settle into relationships primarily because they seem secure. They take jobs because they seem stable. They become rigidly attached to institutions and organizations because they fear letting go. They often support social conventions and political ideals only because they want to belong. They do not want to be the stranger or risk being excluded.

People fear being rejected as unlovable, being revealed as powerless, and being embarrassed as worthless. They avoid taking risks that might unmask them. Unfortunately, unless a person risks being rejected, he never finds a love he can trust. Unless he risks testing his power he does not find a sense of personal security and is never sure of his strength and so spends his life testing his defenses. Unless a person risks losing esteem by doing his best he never finds real appreciation or contentment.

IF YOU DON'T RISK

Not risking is the surest way of losing.

If you do not risk, risk eventually comes to you. There is simply no way to avoid taking a risk.

If a person postpones taking risks, the time eventually comes when he will either be forced to accept a situation that he does not like or to take a risk unprepared. Because risking involves growing, continually postponing risks leaves one childish, fearful and mistrusting. Simply being alive brings a person in contact with opportunities to grow at every level. If you continually shun any stress, you become comfortable with fewer and fewer experiences. Your world shrinks and you become rigid. It takes more and more energy to keep an ever growing number of potential threats from upsetting you. You become committed to being insular. Your life has no direction but is only a reaction to what the world presents to you. And you see whatever the world presents as a threat. Anything that challenges the integrity of your defenses makes you recoil.

If you cannot take risks on your own behalf, you are not your own person. You are your biggest problem.

> If you cannot risk, you cannot grow,
> If you cannot grow, you cannot become
>   your best,
> If you cannot become your best, you cannot
>   be happy,
> If you cannot be happy, what else matters?

WHEN DEFENSES GET IN YOUR WAY

Everyone has defense mechanisms whose purpose is to shield him from the pain of reality. Defenses buy time to reconsider a dangerous situation and to determine the best way to act. Unfortunately, rigid defenses are impervious to pain. They filter and distort reality and we become their prisoners by becoming addicted to the false sense of security they create. Further, when defenses insulate us from feeling a loss, they use up our energy, leaving us less to prevent the loss or to cope with the real world.

Life should be more than a continual defensive operation against pain. We are supposed to feel pain and we are supposed to feel pleasure. Defenses work both ways, limiting pain and joy. A person who is completely "safe" under attack because he has rigid defenses is likely to be paralyzed by those same defenses when he may wish to act or feel. Because defenses were formed by our past fears a defensive person grows little, for he rigidly tries to keep things as they once were. And so a defensive person is never entirely realistic because he never wholly experiences life as it is.

Defenses take the threatening feelings of the moment and put them aside. They distort the world to fit old expectations and allow only the "safe" information to be seen. Some defensiveness is common to everyone, but a rigid person is not free to make new judgments and cannot really protect himself.

How can you be safe if you can't be real? When a defensive person takes a risk, the fears of the present trigger his defenses by tapping into his store of unexpressed past feelings and fears, preventing him from growing or being his best.

YOU CAN GET HURT

In taking a risk it is best to be open about your fears. You are supposed to be afraid when you risk. You fear risking because you must give up something as you leap and you can't always be certain what awaits you when you land. So there are at least two sources of hurt, the real loss implied in every risk and the possible failure of the risk itself.

It is important to remember that you will never take a risk that will solve all of your problems. People with unrealistic expectations never seem to be satisfied. After a while they expect to be let down and so stop trying and end up wallowing in self-pity.

The moment of taking a risk is the most troublesome, when you actually let go and jump free of the bonds of the past, when you ride on the momentum of your leap. That is the time of greatest fear. It's the moment of greatest uncertainty, of taking off and landing. It's the time when people panic and ruin everything. It's the time for a maximum commitment, when your best effort must be made with complete abandon.

A person often loses something merely by deciding to risk. The person who leaves one lover for another may not only fail to win the love he seeks but may never be able to return to the old love. In the same way funds that are invested in a business deal may not only fail to produce the expected profit, they may be lost completely and one's credit may be ruined.

RISKING AND SEPARATION ANXIETY

The fear of taking a leap is familiar to everyone. It is related in part to the survival instinct. It is also similar to separation anxiety. Separation anxiety occurs when children are separated from their parents or when anyone is separated from anything symbolizing security. In normal development these fears are gradually replaced by feelings of trust and self-sufficiency. Yet some children find that going to school produces unbearable anxiety and they develop school phobia. Separation anxiety or its equivalent is also seen when insecure adolescents go to college, when families move, when one takes a new job or even has his office moved down the hall. There are varying degrees of separation anxiety. Anything that signifies the end of the old or the beginning of the new can reawaken these earlier fears of separation.

Separation anxiety is best managed by making plans that help bridge over the uncertain. For example, when a family moves it is a good idea to write ahead to the Chamber of Commerce to inquire about the new neighborhood, its schools, churches, clubs and other resources. The idea is to become as familiar as possible with the new and try to establish some continuity so the family can experience a sense of the familiar on arriving. It is like a traveler touring a country he has read about but has never before visited. He may be homesick, but each new detail he recognizes reinforces his sense of continuity. So, even though the experience of the country is new, it is also familiar and reassuring. The objective is to balance feelings of loss by making new gains, not by avoiding the painful loss.

Some form of separation anxiety, some fear of letting go is present in every act of risking. If it is possible to limit such anxiety, it is helpful to do so, but one should remember that it is impossible to prevent all anxiety in risking. If you wait for all anxiety to pass, the opportunity will have passed, too.

DO OR DIE

No risk worth taking can ever be made completely secure, no matter what technology is at your disposal. The unknown can never be made certain. We can't know everything. We can't even know most of what we are supposed to know.

Many risks fail because they were not taken in time. Too many risks are postponed until unnecessarily elaborate preparations are made. This does not mean that one should say, "Damn the torpedoes, full speed ahead!" That is foolish and self-destructive. Such courage lasts for a brief time. But don't sit back waiting for the perfect moment. It almost never comes.

Success sometimes depends more on the will to leap than on weighing the pitfalls and dangers of failure. The truth is that success falls more to the courageous than to those who understand and plan everything but can't act.

Obviously there must be some balance between reflection and action. There is a point when you lose more by waiting than by doing. And there is a point when you lose more by doing than by waiting.

WITHOUT GUILT

Guilt can also interfere with your ability to take a risk. The most guilt-free risks are those that are made in pursuit of a higher ideal, a better self, or in seeking personal growth and fulfillment. Yet some people feel conflict because they see this as being hurtful to someone else.

You can never be helpful to others until you can help yourself. You can never be giving to another person until you can give to yourself. Some people may object to this view, calling it narrow-minded and selfish, but if you don't take care of yourself, why should anyone else? Anyway, it is your responsibility to make the most of you.

A person who wastes his life denying himself out of a mistaken sense of duty is only diminishing himself and hurting others in the process. The sense of duty such a person rallies behind to justify his self-denial is often exaggerated. He sees his duty as all-consuming because he is afraid to look at his life as a free person. He sees himself as a person with responsibilities toward others first and uses that overblown obligation to excuse his failure to fulfill his own potential and to avoid taking risks.

Because such a martyr does not grow but only becomes trapped, his sacrifice becomes increasingly unrewarding. The people for whom he is sacrificing usually do not share his devotion to his sense of duty or his needs and so are often not grateful for the sacrifices that have been made without their consent. In fact because they have been given so much, others feel entitled to be given to rather than grateful and take their gifts for granted as if they naturally deserve them. Generosity validates entitlement. The giver begins to feel that others are unappreciative and is hurt. Such hurt produces anger and the wish to retaliate by withholding some of the sacrifices that have been made. However, by now the pattern of giving and receiving has become entrenched.

The truth becomes painfully apparent. The person devoted to duty begins to resent giving. He preferred doing for himself in the first place, but felt too ashamed to admit this. His pattern of self-sacrifice, originally begun to win love, have control or seek esteem, is fed by his guilt.

Now he has two problems to overcome. First, he has to come to terms with his own anger at the people he has given to, and with the guilt he feels at withdrawing his insincere giving. For him that is admitting a great deal. The others will not see it his way. They will see the withdrawal of giving as abandonment and the giver will be cast in the role of the villain, which may be unbearably guilt-producing. Second, he must begin the difficult task of examining his own life, discovering what he really wants for himself and why he was unable to take the necessary risks to achieve it before. Finally he must act as directly and honestly as he can, allowing others to be themselves, being his own self without a driving need to shape anyone's destiny but his own.

FINDING YOUR DIRECTION

The purpose of growth is to become better.

Accept your life as a gift.

Accept the responsibility to act in your own best interests.

Believe that if you are a good person what you seek for yourself will also be good, providing you are honest about your needs.

Whenever people avoid acting in their own best interests and shirk the responsibility for their lives, they hold others ransom, demanding appreciation, fulfillment and a sense of completeness by proxy. The truth is that no one can ever fulfill you except you. The way you do that is to take risks. Failure to do this is an act of fear and in the long run harmful to everyone.

A LIFE FREE OF RISK

If you have no anxiety, the risk you face is probably not worthy of you. Only risks you have outgrown don't frighten you. If you create a life that is always comfortable, always without risk, you have only created a fool's paradise. People who hide all fear eventually become stagnant. Many men deny any weakness, fear or vulnerability to show they are strong. They feel obliged to take risks just to prove their strength and do so in "manly" ways without realizing they are only revealing their fears.

A life lived trying to be secure and free of risks eventually becomes a prison. In his later years Howard Hughes tried to insulate himself from decisions, strangers, germs—from risks of all kinds. He rarely ventured out, trusted no one and in the end lived a life that was so horrible that no sane person would envy him. Yet he was ruthless—in protecting himself, in acquiring security, in establishing defenses against risking. He sought the power to protect himself from risks. In avoiding risking he avoided living. How much power does a man have if he is afraid of everything?

HAZARDOUS RISKS

A dynamic life is a life full of risks, but not hazardous risks where a person takes unnecessary chances. Risking everything over the wrong issue avoids as much as never risking at all. When success comes, as it occasionally does to such reckless people, it has little power to confirm love, power or prestige, since so much depended on chance that the risker cannot claim credit for his own action, and so never grows and is only forced to risk again.

Adolescents frequently find themselves in one confusing jam after another and seem to be over their heads in chaotic risking activities all the time. The adolescent's problem is that he has not yet defined himself. He does not know for certain if he is bad or good, weak or strong, a boy or a girl, a boy or a man, a girl or a woman. He regards any evidence that tends to prove his negative view of himself as a threat that must be *actively* repudiated. Adolescents frequently act out their feelings, trying to prove that they are not what they suspect they are. In time an adolescent takes enough risks to establish his identity. Thus he begins to gain the perspective and life experience which enable him to tolerate a view of himself that is not perfect or one hundred percent anything. He learns to accept some parts of himself as good that he formerly may have rejected—like the artistic interest he once considered "sissy."

The adolescent comes of age when he can accept his faults and still believe he is good.

Unfortunately, too many adults have not outgrown their adolescent fears or their adolescent style of handling them. Indeed, many so-called adults are really nothing more than adolescents who have somehow survived into middle age. They remain just as ignorant of their feelings but now use their adult resources to act out their problems more destructively and on a grander scale than before. They are destructive children with an adult's power. They take foolish risks with love, learning nothing from experience and without growing because they do not love themselves. They risk everything for power, but never have enough to feel secure because they feel weak. They risk for esteem but do not like themselves. They still have a need to place their conflicts outside themselves and to take adolescent risks that have adult consequences.

Some people become addicted to the act of risking because it involves facing fear and acting dangerously, which consumes them, arresting their attention. They do not understand that people who value themselves have a goal, realize the effort they must make, and do not leap in the dark. These compulsive riskers have a powerful self-destructive urge that has little to do with the kind of risking we are interested in. They risk till they lose because they want to lose, to be punished, to be restrained, to get attention or to be so out of control that others come to their rescue.

Daniel began to gamble when his wife became pregnant with their first child. Immature and childish himself, he could not bear the prospect of sharing his wife. As feelings of resentment toward the baby grew, he became guilt-ridden and depressed. He could not come to terms with his unmet needs, for his sense of not being given to was deeply rooted. In taking great gambling risks, betting on Sunday's professional football games, Daniel could avoid thinking about his hurt, his anger at the baby and his guilt. His week became bearable only because he could anticipate taking a chance on the weekend.

Daniel was never a big winner or loser until the baby was born, when the rival in his fantasies became a reality. Now he was faced with the object of his anger, and this only made him feel more guilty. *How can I be angry at a helpless baby, my own son?* he thought. The size of his wagers increased until on one especially harrowing Sunday he lost sixty-five thousand dollars, as thirteen out of thirteen bets came crashing in on him as losers.

Daniel was especially unlucky, but at least he survived his risks with his life. Anyone who has served in a war has seen young men so frightened by fear that they take risks simply to avoid thinking about their fear. Pilots who continually volunteer for the most dangerous missions are another example of this. It is as if the person taking unnecessary risks wishes to prove there is nothing to fear by acting as if there is nothing to fear.

The strength of the addiction to the unnecessary risk is determined by the strength of the feeling a person wishes to cover. That feeling can be any feeling at all, but fear and guilt seem most commonly involved. While thrill-seeking riskers may claim that they are seeking a high, they are really running away from a painful feeling. The exhilaration they relish is in forgetting their pain and being temporarily released from an uncomfortable reality.

SHOULD YOU RISK?

When much is at stake even the most carefully planned risks seem unnecessarily hazardous. We do not know if what we are about to do is right. How do you know you wouldn't be better off staying the way you are?

First of all, you *are* the way you *feel*. If *you* are unhappy living your life, *you* have to do something to make your life better. The first risk you must take is to admit that *you* are not where you want to be, that *you* are not feeling the way *you* think *you* should feel, that *you* are not happy.

What can you lose by admitting what you feel? If something in your life is making you unhappy, the only thing you will lose by admitting it is your pretenses. Why wait for something to happen to change your life? Chances are, the events that will change your life will not be in your favor but will merely tip the scales further against you. Waiting to admit your feelings only sets you up to fail.

IT'S NOT TOO LATE

Everywhere you look in your life you'll find problems to solve, risks to take, questions to ask and information to interpret. The well-lived life is spent as the answer to the question, "What am I becoming?" The answer is not given by a single act or statement because your life means more than any one moment or event.

Your life is the direction it takes, not merely the sum of your successes and failures but where you finally decide to go. Sometimes a dismal, dreary life, full of self-denial and withheld feelings, does open up after years of pain. Some people endure much suffering before they are ready to move, before they really believe they must take a chance for something better. When they finally do risk, they know it is what they want and they know what they have to lose.

Some people cope cheerfully and grow more with adversity than others do with success. If your sense of yourself comes from seeing yourself honestly, you will be buoyed up by making your best effort even if it is not always successful. If you take strength from the effort you make, you eventually succeed in growing even if the individual attempts fail. In the end, the only risks that are hazardous are risks where no growth is possible. If you do not believe in yourself, you come to doubt good fortune, and since you have no faith in your ability to acquire what you wish, you have little faith in your ability to hold on to what you have.

Your life should be suggested by your ideals. The way you approach these ideals is to take risks. Your courage to risk comes from the belief that your ideals are worthy.

You would not be where you are now unless you had taken risks, and you will not be where you want to be without risking more.

2

Patterns of Risking

While it is clear that behind every risk there is a fear of a loss, it is sometimes difficult to define that loss or understand what it means.

Each person fears three general kinds of loss in life—the loss of love, control and esteem. Everyone experiences the threat of these losses during childhood. The way one meets these threats and losses as he grows up determines how he will meet similar crises in later years. The pattern that each person finally settles upon for managing them becomes his personality. That is how very basic all of this is.

Each personality is shaped by pain. If we had no pain we would have no defenses and would trust everyone. A growing child is not a complete person, and so his defenses reflect that incompleteness. Thus a child who has not yet acquired language skills will not have verbal defenses but will use more primitive means to block out pain, such as denial.

LOVE

The infant experiences pain when he is hungry. He is relieved when he is fed and comforted. His pain is physical, and he is totally dependent upon someone who can respond to his needs. The infant lives in a world without words where the only negotiable communication is love. The infant does not think, *I am being loved* or *I am not being loved,* but in some subtle way he begins to equate being fed and comforted with being loved. If the infant continually endures pain for too long a period of time before some loving adult comes to his rescue, he may not build strong ties to the outside world, because it seems too threatening, but will focus instead on his own inner world.

DENYING REALITY

Many young children deny reality as their only way to avoid pain. Sometimes when a mother is late with a feeding she finds that her infant has already begun to make sucking motions. Apparently the infant has "imagined" or "remembered" the image of the nipple, and because he cannot differentiate what is real from what is imagined or remembered since this takes a sense of self that has not yet developed, the infant experiences his thoughts as real and sucks at an imaginary nipple. So complete is the infant's ability to do this that a child nursing on an imaginary nipple may act as if he is already fed and refuse the real nipple when it is offered. The act of sucking recalls a previous "memory" of the pain of hunger being alleviated. Such an infant has satisfied his hunger without once relating to the world outside himself. Obviously the infant cannot nurse on imaginary nipples for long without disastrous results.

Whether he knows it or not, the infant traffics in love. If the infant cannot depend upon a mother who meets his needs, whose caring and love draw him out of his internal world and encourage him to trust another person, his ability to relate to any loving figure will be seriously limited in the future. Much, if not most, of our capacity to form a trusting relationship is rooted in this early stage of our lives.

LEARNING TO TRUST

If a child is cared for by a parent who is inconsistent in her nurturing or who is emotionally absent, unaffectionate or passive when she does give, that infant will become an adult who cannot trust or who will continually seek the love he lacked in all the wrong places and in the wrong way. Such children may turn into themselves, denying their pain, or may make such unrealistic demands to be cared for that the world rejects them for their unreasonableness. Thus the world such children later encounter is in part shaped by their early experiences and expectations. Each new experience of rejection reinforces the child's belief that the world is a rejecting and ungiving place where he must either endure pain or hide from it and never trust anyone. Since love is based on trust, such a child finds it difficult to risk anything later on in life that has to do with love. Since he fears he will have to endure pain anyway, why should he stick his neck out and only invite trouble? These children often become adults with one overbearing need: to limit any potential loss of love in their lives. They become dependent on anyone who will show them affection. More than that, they become so twisted by the love of another person that they will alter their lives to ensure that a person loves them, often without questioning whether they want that specific person's love, or if that love is worth having in the first place. They seem unable to nurture a love or keep it when it is offered. When others do pull away, they act helpless, begging others to continue loving them or at least not to abandon them.

RISKING AND THE DEPENDENT PERSON

Betty was a forty-five-year-old married woman whose two children had just grown up and left home. Betty found staying at home alone difficult but was so afraid of starting a life of her own that she could not leave the house. She was trapped. Her whole life had centered around her two sons, neither of whom had accepted her smothering love. Both boys were pleased when, against her tearful protests, their father permitted them to live away at school. For years Betty had dealt with her own needs to be taken care of by caring for her two boys in an overbearing fashion. Betty's husband tolerated her attitude because it occupied her time and kept her from clinging to him.

When the boys left, Betty was on her own for the first time in her life. She had lived in the home of her own overprotective mother until she was sixteen, leaving home for the first time when she married her husband, eighteen years her senior. She had become pregnant almost immediately and then was so preoccupied with the care of her two children that she abandoned any responsibility for her own growth.

Betty's life was torture. In spite of a caring, financially successful husband who was generous and kind to her, she found it impossible to tolerate even small signs of disapproval. Any indication that someone thought her unlovable would throw her into a panic. If a friend disagreed with her she would call all of her other friends to give her side of the argument, seeking support by forcing others to support her. Betty was never open about her feelings, preferring to watch other people and find out what they felt before committing herself.

Betty lived in constant fear of rejection and so could not make up her mind about anything that might reflect on her. She was always beautifully dressed but never purchased anything without checking first with a saleslady in a particular boutique, returning anything that anyone did not seem to like. Because she ventured nothing, nothing Betty did seemed to build her self-confidence.

Betty was never her own person. She was always concerned with the effect that taking a stand would have on other people's opinion of her.

"Will other people like me?" was Betty's motto. To ask why people should like her in the first place would be too threatening for her, for it raised the question "Am I a lovable person?", which her life and all its defenses were constructed to avoid. The answer Betty would give you in a moment if you did ask would be, "Of course I'm lovable," but her actions indicated that she really wasn't sure at all.

Betty began to make demands on her husband that he spend all of his time with her, that he help select her daily wardrobe, even clothes for lounging around the house. Her demands grew more unrealistic the more her husband tried to help her. Betty's husband was originally not very self confident himself; he had been drawn to Betty by the very same dependent needs that were now smothering him.

As he grew and became more self-confident, he no longer needed Betty to be totally dependent on him, even though he had once encouraged it. Because Betty would take no risks, she found herself face to face with the prospect of losing her husband if she did not stop clinging, but all she knew how to do at a time like this was to cling even more.

This case is obviously extreme, but it illustrates how hard it is for a dependent person to take a risk of love. When a person grows up fearing the loss of love as the consequence of any act, his whole life becomes misshapen. Betty's mother was "too giving" and never let Betty take any risks. Betty wanted to take the risk of getting out of her mother's hands but could not do so until she had found someone else who would take Mother's place and hold her even more tightly in his grip.

Betty expected that her husband would never change, but partners can outgrow each other when they outgrow the needs that led them into the relationship in the first place. Both must grow to keep a relationship alive.

Betty could not grow because she had never learned to take a risk on her own. To risk anything implied losing love and affection and simply overwhelmed her. Betty found herself caught between her wish to be taken care of and her fear of being unlovable. Her crisis placed her in a position where she had to answer the old questions she had avoided—"Who am I?" "What am I worth?" and "Does anyone love me?"

For someone who had never confronted these questions, forty-five seemed late in life to begin. Accepting responsibility for herself was to be the first risk Betty would take.

The Fear of Rejection

Any risk that is important for growth will continually reappear until it is settled. If it is not settled there will be no growth.

Everyone fears the loss of love and being unlovable. No

one likes to think of himself as being dependent on others. And yet, those people who are that afraid of offending others tend to become so dependent on others all the time that they can't risk being real.

Arthur was a widely disliked student. He was arrogant and cynical and projected an air of superiority that made others uncomfortable. Arthur was unsure of his own worth, and his insecurity distorted everything he experienced. He wore blinders and insisted that people share his narrow vision. He discussed his point of view as if it were the only one. When someone brought up another position, he simply would not respond. Other people wanted to pull away from him but found his arguments and manner so irritating, so in need of being set straight, that they continually responded to them and in the process rewarded Arthur by paying attention to him. You would think if you spent any time around Arthur that he was the only person in the world who mattered.

Arthur was dependent on people's paying attention to him. He saw any response as the equivalent of being loved. One day a fellow student could stand Arthur's continuous interrupting and scene-stealing no longer, but instead of attacking Arthur's position, which was designed to be attacked, he attacked Arthur as a person who simply was not likable.

"Can't you see," shouted the angry student, "that no one can stand you? That you are a boring phony. That you are not fun to be with and what is more, that you are totally repulsive as a person?"

Arthur became silent, thought for a moment and then quickly continued in the same vein as before. The other student repeated his attack with renewed vigor. "I don't like you. I don't know anyone who does like you."

Over the next few weeks Arthur spent every free moment he could with the student who had attacked him, going out of his way to make friends with him. It was as if Arthur had no choice but to make the other student testify to his worth. It was all right to disagree with Arthur, even vehemently. But to dislike him, that was something different. The other student had said he was unlikable, and that hit home, for it was what Arthur secretly believed and dreaded. Arthur was suddenly totally dependent on others for the way he felt about himself.

The problem with both Arthur and Betty was that they had never been able to see themselves as persons who were both good and bad and still had worth. They could not tolerate accepting anything negative in themselves, which would justify someone's rejecting them. With these feelings of dependency there was also a need to appear perfect, although neither was even close.

The threat of the loss of a parent's love and the dread that one is not lovable are the underlying fears behind all risks of love. No parent is perfect, nor is any likely to be, and so all of us are at one time or another deeply involved in some uncertainty over being loved and being lovable.

> When you deny what is real,
> When you hide from life's pains,
> When you shut out the world,
> Only fantasy remains.

CREATING YOUR BEST LIFE

When we make a serious mistake, especially doing something we value highly, our failure colors the way we see ourselves. The evidence a person uses to back up his opinion of himself is gathered selectively with a prejudiced view in mind. There is often as much negative as positive evidence available, and so a person can write the story of his life supporting either view, depending on how he feels.

Why not write the best possible story of your life? Look at the most promising parts of your past for reinforcement instead of allowing yourself to be undermined by the worst. Failures are part of everyone's past. When people have a lot of negative experience, much of it turns out to be the same mistake repeated over and over again. This is not proof that life will always be bad. Problems are solvable if you are willing to see yourself in a new light.

Expecting rejection only fills you with fear and makes you act as the least desirable version of yourself, causing you to make other people uncomfortable. If they do reject you, you cannot be sure they are rejecting you for yourself. You can always pretend people are stupid and don't understand, but when you want to be accepted, it still hurts.

No one can ever really grow or come to terms with his fears of rejection until he risks being rejected as himself. Only when you risk exposing your true feelings can you ever be accepted. It is only with that experience of acceptance that you can become independent of other people's opinion of your worth and learn to feel worthy just because you are you.

> Independence is the proper goal.
> Learn to love yourself,
> To need love, but not be governed by that
>   need alone,
> To be able to love without fear,
> To risk rejection but not invite it.

These risks cannot be taken until one is willing to accept all of himself, the weaknesses and shortcomings with the strengths. Then whatever rejection one may encounter in life is not seen as proof that one is unlovable, but that one is human.

CONTROL

At the next step in development a child is concerned with mastering his own body and risking the loss of control over his bodily functions and his negative feelings. Although this phase of development is the one in which a child learns to use controls, the fear behind losing control is again the threat of the loss of love. Specifically, the child fears losing control and soiling himself because he fears disappointing his mother, getting her angry and losing her love by being "bad."

Since control is the major issue at this time, anything that can be controlled can become the focus of a problem. The child often equates losing control of his body with losing control of his feelings. The way in which a child learns to manage the risk of losing control of his body shapes his response to potential losses of control later in life.

The child's greatest fear at this stage is still losing mother's love by not being lovable, just as it was earlier. If the child did not have a secure infancy and did not learn to feel loved, it is unlikely he will be able to master the issue of control successfully, since the underlying issue is the same. To repeat, unresolved issues in life always come back to haunt you.

Again, exposure to pain molds the way defenses are shaped. A person's armor is formed by his need to protect himself and is thickest where his fears are most concentrated. While the infant's defenses serve to deny his pain—by withdrawing into himself, shutting out reality or identifying with his protector—the older child tries to control his pain. He uses his newly developed language skills and reason to explain his pain, to justify or rationalize why he is out of control. He uses words to place the blame away from him. His goal is to control the situation so mother will not be angry with him.

THE FEAR OF LOSING CONTROL

It is difficult to learn from a risk if one is always trying to stay in control. Although danger can be limited by prudent planning, some loosening of controls is needed to have forward motion.

When a person fears losing control, any possible weakness appears as a serious threat, and even irrelevant uncertainties can consume his energy. The perspective of what is important becomes lost in trivial fears.

People who are concerned with control are always concerned with power. They often have grand ideas that seem to have roots in the real world but are really compensation for their fear of being out of control. Often their grandiose ideas soothe the pain of being unable to control another person's love or of being powerless or inadequate. Often, the need to stay in control becomes the direct cause of a situation's falling apart. Such people fear losing control so much they try to control everything and see anything that acts freely or beyond their control as a potential threat.

When a person is concerned with control, taking any risk causes great anxiety. Such people fear losing the power, influence or strength to ensure that others will love them and think of them as worthy. They think of being strong as being right and being in control as being good. Controlling people seldom deal with what really bothers them; mostly they deal in symbols, where doing one thing stands for something else.

What Can You Control?

Each of us must learn to put the issue of control into proper perspective. What can you control in this world? Few things can be controlled completely and very little that is worthwhile can be more than superficially managed.

You can control money, property—that is, things. You control them best by possessing them and guarding them, but if you act too rigidly you can lose. You really cannot control people or feelings. You can try to manage feelings, but you can't take a feeling and shut it out without running the risk of that feeling's returning and demanding to be expressed, perhaps in a way which is entirely out of your control. Feelings need to be expressed. That is their nature. When painful feelings are held in, more and more energy is required to restrain them, until they eventually imprison the controlling person in his own defenses.

> You cannot control love,
> You cannot control tomorrow,
> You cannot control the past,
> You can only live honestly now.

If There Were No Rules

When a person takes a risk, he does not abandon all controls, although a person who is not used to taking risks, who prefers the same routine day after day, tends to see any change as a loss of control. Some people find it difficult to be in a situation without rules, limits or clear-cut directions. They try to control every situation as a way of controlling their own feelings.

If people were left alone without rules and allowed to fulfill their own needs, life would go on pretty much the same, except there would be a lot more time to relax. People wouldn't be continually checking to see how they were doing, how much they were worth or how they felt. But, like it or not, controlling people wrote most of the rules and regulations in this world. Controlling people secretly fear that they and mankind are not basically good and need regulation to keep in step. No wonder life can feel stifling at times, especially since controlling people are also the people who enforce the rules.

A person concerned with controls is often out of touch with his own feelings. If you want to understand how you are, you need only ask how you feel. But for people who are concerned with keeping feelings and everything else under control, that is an enormous risk all by itself. It is the risk they always avoid.

The alternative to being rigidly in control is not to be out of control but simply to be free: to flow with your feelings wherever they go, accepting yourself as worthwhile and good, and since you are good, realizing that your feelings, even your negative feelings, cannot be entirely bad. Feelings are merely your emotional reaction to your experience of living. Expressing feelings without the restriction of stifling controls is the process of living fully.

Taking the Wrong Risk

Rodger was a playboy, in his father's estimation. He never made much out of his opportunities, always taking the easy road, more interested in fun than in work. That would be his father's description, and it would be wrong even though it could easily be documented.

Rodger's father, "Irish" Kelly, was the hardest hitting

tackle in the history of the Harvard football team. He was also the most ambitious, wildest underclassman who ever graced the brick-and-ivy Harvard Yard. Irish went into the family textile business just before the war and invested his considerable energy producing wartime supplies for the government. The Kellys prospered. Irish married a woman who spoke with an affected Boston accent and had a sizable Brahmin fortune, and in short order Rodger was born.

Although Irish detested his wife's aristocratic background, it did not stop him from investing her money, sometimes wisely and sometimes impulsively, with disastrous results. Fortunately for the Kelly clan, the government had plenty of business to offer, and Irish's investment indiscretions were absorbed with little effect.

As Rodger grew, it became clear that he was his mother's child. He was sent to the same private schools that Irish had attended. He did poorly but was passed along out of deference to his father's sizable contributions to the alumni fund. Rodger was a sensitive boy who could not stand being compared unfavorably to his father, who he found had been everywhere he went before him and had always done well.

Rodger was never a playboy; he was, more accurately, a drifter. He could not be aggressive about anything because his aggression was held back by defenses that were put in position to contain Rodger's anger at his father for never loving him, putting him down, and publicly ridiculing him. When Rodger was twenty, he went to work for Father, running the least profitable of Father's businesses, the failure Father had created with his wife's money. Somehow this was poetic justice to Father. Rodger, he felt, deserved no more than an outdated company that ran at a loss and that he could neither sell nor reorganize.

The only reason the company was kept was that it supplied another of Father's companies with materials.

Rodger hated work, but every day he came in, sat in his office and listened to the advice of Father's associates. Rodger's hatred for Father seemed to grow over the years but was never expressed. When Father died unexpectedly when Rodger was thirty-two, Rodger found himself in charge of a huge company and in control for the first time.

All those years when Rodger was running the failing division, he had appealed to Father to invest more capital and update the plant. Father always refused, saying it was all Rodger deserved, that he could do no better if he tried. Rodger swallowed his pride and waited. Now his advisors suggested he sell the smaller division and work with the more profitable companies.

Rodger would have none of it. He was in charge and he had a bone to pick. He wanted to prove to everyone that he was right and that his father had been wrong. All the failing division needed, Rodger reasoned, was some hard work and some capital. The reason people were not buying the product, according to Rodger, was simply that the product was not well advertised. Acting against his advisors, Rodger funneled large amounts of money from his profitable businesses into the failing division.

A whole new side of Rodger's personality emerged. He seemed aggressive and confident. He acted clearly, without ambivalence, and the people who worked for him might almost have been impressed if they had not known in their hearts that his attempts to rescue the failing company placed their jobs in jeopardy. Rodger knew the failing company well. In fact, it was the only part of the business he understood. What he did not understand was his need to appear better than Father, to appear right, to be vindicated after all those years. Further, Rodger did not understand his great anger at Father or how difficult it was for him to express it.

As he became more involved with the managing of the company, Rodger became rigid and set in his ways. It was as if his personality had been transformed. His former devil-may-care self was replaced by a nitpicking, detail-examining Scrooge who became stingy in allocating funds to all divisions except the one he had a need to make flourish.

A large advertising campaign brought much publicity to the failing company, but no matter how much he advertised, sales were still as poor as they had always been. Rodger streamlined the plant, brought in new people, who, because the economy was faltering, were willing to take any job they could find.

With his warehouses full of the product to the rafters, Rodger needed to go into debt to meet a payroll for the first time. He became unnerved and found it impossible to concentrate on anything but saving the failing company. Every profit the other divisions made was invested in it. Rodger reviewed every note, chart, sales slip and production order. He was on top of the most insignificant details of the company, ignoring the weakening position of his other businesses. In truth, the failing division was the only part of the company Rodger felt comfortable controlling. He exerted control where he could, not where it was needed. His need to control became greater than anything else, and the more the company faltered the more urgently he poured money into it. He would not listen to reason or alter his plans.

When his advisors demanded that he meet with them to reconsider his plans, Rodger reluctantly agreed. The bank demanded payment on some of his notes and threatened to put him into receivership if he did not begin to act more prudently. It was already too late. Rising interest rates had eaten into whatever profits had not been poured down the drain of the smaller company.

Rodger had been able to act unambivalently and to risk for the first time in his life. In so doing, he destroyed Father's business in an attempt to make his own division prosper, to show everyone after all that he was not the failure Father claimed he was. His anger at Father came out in this controlled way. No one could ever accuse Rodger of being disinterested or lacking effort and drive. Rodger emulated Irish down to the last ounce of bravado. The reason he could act without hesitation in destroying Father's company was that in some way he was also destroying himself. The self-punitive nature of his risk took away his guilt and made it possible for him to act angrily. It was a symbolic standoff between his old anger at Father and his present guilt.

When a person tries to control feelings by controlling things, his judgment becomes clouded by his incomplete understanding of his emotions. His feelings remain hidden but still exert a destructive influence on his life, which easily gets out of control and, as in Rodger's case, is not easily open to the suggestion of others.

Such a person tries to apply whatever controls he can, simply to reassure himself that he is not powerless and may persist in a self-destructive course of action even when the results seem opposite to what he claims he wants. Such people dread losing power more than anything else. That is understandable because they seek to control the outside world rather than looking at themselves and dealing with the feelings within.

Unfortunately, unless these people can learn to deal with feelings directly, the world they experience will always seem on the verge of going out of control. Some fears, some pain, some anger must be felt if one is to grow and to be free.

ESTEEM

As the child grows he becomes concerned with esteem, with the way other people regard him. He thinks about the questions: "Am I good, Am I better, Am I best?" He tries to answer these questions by his actions. The child also becomes concerned with his identity. "Am I like Mommy or Daddy?" he asks. He fears that if he falls in esteem then he is out of control and not lovable.

If the issue of esteem sounds like a cover for the old issue of being lovable once again, it is.

As the infant first denies pain and later excuses his failure to control himself, the older child tries to pretend that reality is different from what he experiences. This pretense is the way the older child deals with the threats of pain. He may say, "I am not afraid," or "You can't hurt me," and put on a show of bravery.

It is hard to take a risk if you deny the threat or make excuses for failure. It is equally difficult to take a risk when you pretend not to care. You cannot adequately prepare for a risk when you pretend you aren't really interested in taking the risk, or that you are just along for the ride. This pretense serves the purpose of saving face, which is what the person concerned with esteem values most. He may pretend to risk only to admit later that he really didn't try and that he didn't do his best. Such people always hold a little effort in reserve as balm for their anticipated failures. People who pretend in this way are often good actors and get other people stirred up, drawn into their affairs, expressing their feelings for them.

STAGE FRIGHT AND RISKING

Clara was a music student who had not really committed herself to a career as a performer. She saw herself as a femme fatale and went out on dates with older men and wore an ostrich boa around her neck at a time when her roommates were wearing jeans and dating contemporaries. Clara dated men in show business who were sexually demanding and expected a great deal of their brief encounters. When, after a liaison with a man who owned a small nightclub, Clara was offered a chance to perform on stage, she panicked and abruptly broke off the relationship, pretending that the club had terrible acoustics.

Soon after, a similar situation developed in which she convinced a producer that she wanted a part in a musical. After an especially hot and heavy evening that seemed more like a Hollywood movie scene from the nineteen-thirties than it did like reality, Clara got a minor singing role—but just before going on stage she lost her voice.

Clara could not take a risk that really mattered to her. She could only pretend. She could become sexually involved with these men from that world of glitter, but she did not consider her involvement real because she did not consider herself real. Life was only a game. Getting up and performing as herself, being seen, being looked at and measured and judged was a threat she simply could not meet. Rather than appearing as herself, she backed away.

People who pretend they are not really involved in the risks they take live lives that are often tumultuous. Since they pretend that they are not really involved, what they do lacks their emotional participation and so is often out of their control. They act out their feelings unawares, sometimes as if they were another character. In so doing they often seem histrionic, a bit put on.

Such people often take enormous risks in spite of themselves. Like Clara, they are often provocative. Their feelings, although concealed from themselves, excite the people they play to and spur them into action. Thus, situations often get out of control, since people take their displayed emotions at face value. They disappoint others and, as should come as no surprise, create a great deal of anger. When they are finally confronted and pinned down to account for their provocative behavior, they reply innocently, "Who, me?"

PRETENDING AS A DEFENSE MECHANISM

While most people who use pretense to handle fear are not as obvious as Clara, their playacting still poses a problem for them. It still keeps them from confronting what is real and from growing to a stronger position, where they will not need to be so defensive. Many people spend their lives playing roles that are only subtly different from the way they would be if they weren't acting. They don't even notice the difference between acting and being themselves and cannot admit they are role playing even when it is pointed out. They suppress their real feelings and do not recognize them as their own. Should their real feelings ever surface, they are likely to disown them, fail to recognize them or carry on the pretense, "Who, me? Don't be ridiculous." The person playing a role characteristically rejects his real self when it appears, because the risk of being responsible for what he is or feels overwhelms him.

At no time is this any more obvious or painful than when such people are confronted with feelings of grief. It is difficult to pretend that a loved one was not important to you when he was. In grief, negative feelings toward the deceased must eventually be expressed. People who pretend not to have negative feelings find themselves suppressing their anger at being left alone, abandoned or having their love taken away and so never quite resolve their grief, even though they may go into hysterics, acting out what they cannot experience.

You can pretend you do not care
But then you feel no joy.
You can pretend you do not feel
But then your sadness becomes trapped
    within.
You can pretend you are not you
But then everything seems like a dream.

You can only live your life as you.
If you want the esteem you believe you
    deserve,
You must risk all your failures as yourself.

PATTERNS OF LIVING

Unresolved problems in childhood produce unmet needs in the character of the adult who follows.

The child who is deprived of love becomes insecure in his adult relationships. He is fearful of having other people leave him. He wishes to possess the people he loves because he doubts his own worth and specialness and with it his ability to love. And so he cannot give of himself.

The child who has problems with control becomes an adult who tries to control his and others' feelings rather than risk losing their affection or allowing them to act freely. He fears losing control and finds it difficult to accept himself as imperfect.

The child who has difficulties accepting and feeling comfortable with his identity becomes an adult who wishes to impress others or compete with them. In other words, he defines himself by others' reactions to him rather than from within.

All people wish to possess, control or impress others when they feel stressed by the threat of danger, simply because each person bears the imprint of his own childhood experience. No one ever had all his needs met or grew up without pain or fear. Great fears make one feel helpless and childlike and therefore less able to act responsibly. Knowing how emotions interfere with judgment, understanding how they can sidetrack one is helpful.

The following guide will show you how these unresolved feelings express themselves in your life.

ISSUES	DEPENDENT OR POSSESSIVE POSITION	CONTROLLING POSITION	COMPETITIVE OR IMPRESSING POSITION
When I am afraid of losing love, control or esteem	I deny the danger or panic	I act brave or afraid of something else	I pretend not to care
When I am hurt by losing love, control or esteem	I make others feel guilty or responsible for me by acting helpless	I hold my anger in and try to seem invincible	I pretend to be happy or overplay my injury in a dramatic way
When I am angry over my hurt	I throw a tantrum	I bury it and do nasty little things that are hard for others to define	I make a public display bringing embarrassment to the people who hurt me
When I feel guilty over my anger	I hurt myself and let others know, seeking sympathy	I make painful reparations and deny myself pleasure	I seek out forgiveness publicly by running myself down, and I overdo it to get others to restrain me

The risks that every child faces in growing up—to risk being independent, being free and being oneself without pretense—remain the risks that we must all spend our lives taking and resolving. To be independent and loving, to be free in expressing feelings and one's own person are the characteristics of being a healthy person. They are the requirements for being real and for knowing the only happiness you can ever experience and maintain.

We all try to deny the hurt of a love taken away, to make excuses when events seem out of control and to pretend we don't care when we are embarrassed, for that is how we were brought up. Our goal in life should be to free ourselves from these avoiding tactics and to solve the problems in our lives by dealing with risks straightforwardly.

3

The Moment of Risk

Passing in an automobile illustrates the dangers involved in taking other risks. Passing is the most dangerous moment in driving, when most fatalities occur. The driver most likely to be killed is the one who hesitates, loses his nerve and can neither accelerate nor apply his brakes. He cannot follow through on a commitment to act.

Even though the stages move quickly in passing, preparing, committing and moving on, all the elements of risking are there. Recognizing the need to risk and deciding to risk, making a commitment to take a chance, reaching the point of no return and completing the risk are all features of passing. The discussion of passing that follows is intended as a metaphor and is offered as a useful device for learning more about risking.

When you think about it, whether you seek a promotion to advance your career, try to win the affections of someone you care for, consider buying a house, want to introduce a new product for the fall line, expand the business to the West Coast, experiment with a new sexual technique, try to get into pictures, get a divorce, tell off your mother-in-law—or if you want to do anything else in life that implies getting ahead, becoming better or growing—you are in a passing situation.

Sometimes the obstacle you're trying to overcome is another person. Sometimes it's a set of social conventions. Sometimes it's the influence others have on you or the restrictions that your own narrow-minded expectations have placed on you. No matter what you are breaking away from, the act of passing symbolizes the moment of truth, leaving the position you've grown accustomed to, forging ahead and confronting the unknown.

Passing is always a risk. And, even when the risk is known, the variables are so many and they change so quickly that you can be overwhelmed as much by the act of passing as by the particular risk you take. Understanding the variables involved helps.

It is impossible to discuss all of the variables in every risk, but the example of passing can be expanded, with minor changes, and applied to almost any other risking situation.

PASSING, THE WRONG WAY

It is three o'clock, Friday afternoon, densely overcast and threatening to rain. Jay Bergman, a manufacturer's representative in housewares, has just decided that he is not going to make a sale today and is quitting early. After stopping for a few drinks, Jay decides to try to make it home before rush-hour traffic. He takes the wheel of his car, which is nine thousand miles overdue for its scheduled servicing, and heads home. His tires are nearly bald. His car's acceleration is sluggish, probably because his spark plugs are oil-fouled and his engine is losing compression. Although the company pays for the car's upkeep, Jay pockets the money.

It is a dreary end to a dreary week. Bergman's life is at a standstill, a repetitive bore. Jay is just getting by, but the price he pays to tolerate the boredom is to become less sensitive to the world. He just wants to get through the week and pay his bills. He can feel the two Martinis. He's starting to relax.

The rains come. Traffic is slowing down on the highway. Drivers put their headlights on. "Damn," Bergman says aloud, "stuck in traffic." He decides to get off the highway and takes a side road, one he does not know as well. "Maybe I can make time there," he says.

Traffic is faster on the side road, although it is not as safe. There are puddles everywhere; some extend nearly across the midline. The rains intensify. Visibility gets worse. The road is changing—winding one minute, open the next. It is a two-lane road, and oncoming traffic is heavy. Bergman finds himself trapped behind a large truck, which loses speed on the hills, slowing down to a crawl approaching the crest.

Bergman feels locked in. He is worse off than he was on the highway. "I never should have done this," he says. "I would be home now if I had stayed put before. The tie-up was probably just a small bottleneck. This whole damn week has been like this. I can't seem to do anything right. I can't get ahead anywhere. I wish I were home watching television."

Bergman is restless and looking for an opportunity to pass the truck. Spaces in traffic to pass seem few and far between. Bergman pulls up close to the truck and tailgates, angering the truck driver. After he misses several opportunities to pass, Bergman's frustration and impatience build. He decides to move at the very next opening he sees. One appears. Bergman accelerates and pulls out into the oncoming lane, noticing for the first time as he does so that he is on a hill. His car sputters. He is almost even with the truck, which is trying to maintain speed to make the hill. The truck driver is still angry at this jerk in the compact car, who has been bugging him for the past ten miles, and is not especially eager to give him part of the road.

The lights of an oncoming car suddenly appear over the hill. The road is too narrow for the cars to make it by safely. Jay's car cannot pull ahead. When he depresses the accelerator to the floor, the car only misfires. Jay looks to the truck driver for help, but only sees a man shaking his head, mouthing the words, "Stupid bastard." That's all Jay needs. He is unnerved. He hesitates, depresses his brakes, swerves and spins out of control. His car goes off the road. Just before he hits a tree Jay says, "How could this happen to me?"

Bergman tried to pass while in a dreary, unalert frame of mind. He had been drinking, buoyed up by a false sense of security. He was tired, unable to respond. He was rushing, on unfamiliar roads in poor condition. His chronic failure to assume responsibility for himself was reflected in his car's being out of shape. His feelings of frustration and impatience led him to antagonize the driver he had to pass, making him reluctant to give Bergman a break. Bergman was his own agent of destruction.

A great deal can be learned by examining the various steps in successful passing and applying the principles to other risks. The following schematic approach will help organize some of the chaos and unpredictability that attend every risk. For the purpose of this discussion, risking is broken down into three phases—preparing, committing and completing.

PHASE ONE: PREPARING

Step 1: RECOGNIZING YOUR NEED TO RISK

This step varies from person to person. Some drivers are content to stay in line, barely moving even when they have a specific purpose. Others feel frustrated merely to be behind another car, even a fast-moving one and even when they are just out for a Sunday drive. Some people always need to be in motion. Others are afraid to move and are glad to have excuses to stay where they are. But when you find yourself in a dangerous situation—such as being trapped behind an unpredictable or drunken driver or a car with a precariously secured load on its roof—you have to get out of the way.

YOU'RE IN DANGER

In some way recognizing the need to risk is always threatening because a person must admit that he is not as safe or that he is not getting where he wants as fast as he wants. In a love relationship both partners often pretend they are getting along better than they really are because admitting one is unhappy with his relationship implies that he must do something about it. It's the *do something* that is so frightening. Do what, when, how? And it's also painful to admit you have played a role in causing a problem or have hurt another person.

Discovering the need to risk power, position or authority can be paralyzing because it upsets the stability that power, position and authority were supposed to ensure.

Realizing he must invest more money in a venture can panic an executive who wants to avoid making a bigger commitment or test his judgment. Suddenly he must decide whether to place more valuable resources in jeopardy to protect his investment or stand pat in the face of danger. When a businessman ignores a real need to risk, the day when he will be in deeper trouble will come to him on its own. Many businessmen are afraid to admit danger because they fear revealing earlier bad decisions and dread making another. They try to pretend that the threat will go away, so they will not be uncovered.

The successful businessman is realistic. He stays on top of the situation without pretending that business is better than it is just to feel good. He takes a little distance and views his business operation objectively. If something is wrong, he wants to know about it when it's easiest to fix mistakes. He does not hide out of shame or guilt or fear of embarrassment.

FEAR MAKES YOU READY

Similarly, the student who refuses to admit his own shortcomings when studying for an exam is unlikely to strengthen his weaknesses. If you pretend you don't need to prepare, it will be difficult to make your best effort and, should you fail, you can only pretend you didn't care.

To risk implies taking action. Of course, you can just sit where you are, afraid to take a chance, doing nothing, waiting for deliverance. Maybe getting ahead is not that important to you. Maybe it's too important. Maybe you don't want to risk failing. It's your decision. But if you want to reach your goals, you will have to overcome the obstacles that stand in your way. You either risk, face a slow inevitable failure or change goals.

STEP 2: DECIDING TO RISK

This next step is harder to take.

Everyone knows people who have openly admitted they are dissatisfied with their lives, love, work or careers, yet still can't seem to decide to do anything about it. In the passing example the driver alone is responsible for his vehicle's actions. It is his job to decide if, where and when to pass. Just as you must decide what to do next to get where you want.

People who continually postpone decisions cannot risk without encountering old, unresolved risks from their pasts. Imagine how hard it is for a person who has never allowed himself to get close to anyone before to decide whether to become romantically involved with another person. When his old fears return, he again postpones getting close to another person.

THE FEAR OF EXPOSURE

Many business people feel powerful making little decisions, but large risks paralyze them. They dread injuring the company, hurting its credit rating or overextending its capital. Often a businessman cannot risk because he fears losing control or making bad decisions that will prove him unfit. You can't evaluate a list of potential business gains honestly and act decisively if you believe any failure will reveal your incompetence. When personal issues become the main factors in making a business decision, a safe outcome is unlikely. A person who needs to prove his personal worth by taking a business risk is risking the wrong thing in the wrong place.

For this reason many businessmen try to avoid risks

and, instead, try to give an impression of stability and strength by taking a rigid stand. They act confident, forceful and determined, but until they feel accepting of themselves, they cannot be sure if their risks are necessary or merely camouflage for old personal fears. You can't make a good business decision if you don't understand why you fear making it.

KEEPING PERSPECTIVE

All of our secret hopes come to the surface at the moment we decide to give up the old and the known. We feel free not only to leap but to allow our daring to spur us on to risk even more. We sense our power as we finally decide to move, but our soaring hopes can lead us to overextend our goals dangerously in midair, at which point we have little control, for we are riding on momentum alone.

So it's important to make a plan for initiating the risk and following it through, as well as an alternative plan in case of danger. Merely thinking about bailing out is often all it takes to make a plan you can fall back on in an emergency.

GETTING YOUR BEARINGS

Some businessmen have great difficulty making alternate plans. They tend to put all their time and money in one effort when they risk. This full commitment may be helpful to attain success when the original decision is correct, but it does not give much room for pulling out intact if you happen to be wrong. In business it is crucial to analyze your downside risks and limit losses as much as possible. Not to know how you can lose, not to be aware of the earliest danger signs is simply to gamble. For this reason businessmen, especially investors, often rely on business services that offer predictions and on business indicators that point out trends. However, most business indicators are vague and can only be used to support or weaken decisions that have, for all practical purposes, already been made. A good businessman always decides to risk on his own judgment, not because some indicator has suddenly reached a particular level. Blaming some index is merely a way of avoiding responsibility. Acting at one point of a particular business indicator is really risking on your own; after all, you decided to act then, no one forced you.

A business decision is only as strong as the person who makes it. Of all the variables that go into making a successful business venture, none is as important as the vision and experience of the person in charge. A strong leader's view shapes the company's goals. His decisions resolve conflicts, point out what is necessary, eliminate what is unimportant. He decides mindful of failure but not paralyzed by fear. His flexibility allows him to adapt to change even when that means admitting he was wrong.

Whatever your reasons for deciding to risk, if they are not arrived at by honest acceptance of yourself—who you are and where you are going—your risk becomes increasingly dangerous. You will be overwhelmed by your fears and dishonesty at the very point you must make a clear commitment.

PHASE TWO: COMMITTING

STEP 3: COMMITTING TO PASS—INITIATING THE RISK

This is the step where you put your plans into action.

You have looked at the road; you understand your need and have decided to act. The time is right. You step on the gas and go. The commitment to pass is crucial, giving you strength, a point of resolve and courage to overcome the fears ahead. When you make a commitment, you take action. The risk is on!

The moment of commitment is especially difficult. A process has begun. As you accelerate, your perception changes. Events seem to be taking place more rapidly. Your sense of time and distance is constantly changing. It's hard to get your bearings. Fear also makes time appear to slow down and adds to the disorientation, which in turn creates more fear.

NOW IT'S REAL

Often when a person makes a commitment and puts his plans into action, he begins to understand his risk for the first time. The woman who for years has thought of leaving her husband finally commits herself by announcing her intention to go. Even though she has anticipated her husband's reaction, she has no idea what will happen until she actually tells him. As she does, her guilt and his hurt flood over her. She suddenly knows what it feels like to be the injuring party. He is crying. She feels cruel. He becomes agitated. She is beside herself. She would like events to proceed in reality the way they did in her fantasy. The same old patterns of pain and entrapping guilt that characterized their relationship before appear again. The old problems, which led to the need to risk, come out in the open and make themselves known at the time the commitment is made.

HOW ARE YOU DOING? HOW DO YOU KNOW?

A businessman often does not know how he is doing until some time after he makes a commitment. He has both an advantage and a disadvantage over other riskers, because he can make his commitment in a cooler, less emotional atmosphere, but his results take time. He can direct his forces to his goal slowly and in an organized way. He orders the necessary retooling and the raw materials. He has selling information printed and distributed to his sales force. He builds up the employees' enthusiasm, gets them prepared emotionally for the new line and fills them with hope and promise. And finally he commits himself to a marketing test and waits, before he receives sales results that he can interpret.

His success may not be as great as hoped for. It may be spotty with some salesmen reporting huge sales, others less. Whom does he listen to? The salesmen who are successful or those who are not? How much does he rely on his judgment, independent of early results? He knows that statistics and figures can be stretched to support any view. He can rationalize that the salesmen with poorer responses were not as good as the others or that a full advertising campaign will improve results. In the end, he relies on the strength of his original commitment.

Just after a business commitment is made, little feedback from the marketplace may be available. The first response comes from employees who may not have the desire or the courage to move ahead. The comments that are heard are often unreliable, based on envy or fear. Some are made by those company men who support blindly. The business decision maker is very much alone until his idea becomes established, and he must be prepared to borrow courage from his convictions and give support to his workers, who may not be party to his vision. Even in big companies the risk taking and the sustaining are often the work of one man.

You cannot pass if the oncoming lane is filled, no matter how committed you are to passing.

But neither can you pass in a clear oncoming lane if you are not committed.

STEP 4: THE POINT OF NO RETURN

In every risk there is a point of no return. The commitment is made. You are picking up speed. You pull into the oncoming lane. You are eye to eye with the other driver. You can't go back.

Should you now discover that you are suddenly in danger, you save yourself by moving ahead, not by applying the brakes. You have no choice but to accelerate, sound your horn and create a safe place for yourself. People get killed when they pass without really being committed and so hesitate at the point of no return. It is the possibility of getting cold feet at this critical moment that makes all risking so dangerous.

GATHERING POWER

When a person builds to the point of no return, he must first gather momentum and power and also reassert his conviction in his purpose. That stored power consists of accepting goals and coming to terms with your need to move on. All of that momentum is breathtakingly fragile, easily undermined by fear or doubt. You may doubt that you know what to do, why you should do it, how or when. The fears that may suddenly drain your momentum vary with the risk taken.

UNDERLYING FEARS

In risks of love people fear losing the love of others, they fear being rejected, being hurt, being hurtful and they also fear losing love for themselves and for the other person. They fear falling out of love, losing their lovability and losing their worth as persons.

In risks of power—that is, risks of business, money, influence and control—people fear losing whatever they use to control others, but underlying all these is the fear of being weak, bad, angry, impotent, unfit, cruel or vulnerable.

In risks of esteem people fear losing face, reputation. They dread being embarrassed, shown up, made fun of or ridiculed. They fear appearing diminished to others. They fear having their true feelings made public, especially when they have not come to terms with them. People who take risks of esteem often panic at the moment of truth. This is the basis for most stage fright—the fear of performing, of being seen, of being counted, measured, evaluated or judged. Any act of risking in which one seeks to be judged worthy or excellent can create great fear. Such fear is vital to anyone who wishes to do his best, for it prepares one for stress. The best way to discover one's identity is to seek a high goal with all one's energy.

When a person chooses to gain esteem by being competitive, he's just avoiding confronting himself. Competitive people try to be better than others rather than to be their best selves. At the moment of truth such people are frequently overcome by the realization that they are not and never will be better than everyone else. This detracts from their conviction and gives them cold feet, even when they have the ability to win.

The point of no return varies with each pass, each person and each risk. It is illusory. You cannot mark it down on the road, circle a date on a calendar or point to a moment in a relationship when it occurs. The point of no return is the moment before which the risk can be aborted and after which it can't. After reaching the point of no return, there is a feeling of closure, the beginning of resolution. The risk has been taken and now it's win or lose; you can't back out.

PHASE THREE: COMPLETING

STEP 5: COMPLETING THE RISK

Once the driver passes the point of no return, he glides back into line and is on his way, feeling exhilarated, powerful, and sometimes a little shaken, just happy to have arrived all in one piece. There is a danger that the driver's alertness may now slacken. Much care is still needed. The road is always unpredictable and speed still kills. The driver must adapt to his new position and anticipate the next danger on the road.

LEAVING THE OLD

For dependent people, the difficulty of risking is in leaving the familiar behind. It may be that the old home, the old job, old friends and lovers suddenly begin to take on a soft, idealistic glow when they are abandoned, making them seem better than they were. When a dependent person takes a risk that requires him to be more self-sufficient, the past seems brighter because someone else was caring for him.

People who risk for love often feel ambivalent about fulfilling themselves, especially when they hurt others. They struggle to remain true to their conviction and not yield to guilt. The pain of guilt is one of the consequences of such risks. Should one realize unexpectedly that his new life or love is not perfect, the guilt may not be offset by positive feelings, and the risker may wish to return to the past. The risk of love that allows a person to feel free of possessiveness and his own person is most likely to be successfully completed.

ADAPTING

The problem in completing a risk of control is not a lack of resolve but inflexibility. The businessman grows attached to his methods when he discovers they work and tends to adopt them as standard procedure. In so doing, he creates a need for future risks when he will have to readapt to the changing world. He would be much better off being flexible, realizing that nothing ever stays the same for long. He will have to risk again when his method becomes outdated or is no longer appropriate. Many businesses take one good idea and reapply it over and over. If the businessman cannot adapt, the efforts required to stay the same eventually make business unprofitable.

The businessman must not only deal with his own fears, but with those of his employees who fear change and tend to be even more rigid, to the point of subverting the company's efforts. The best plan is one that is always adapting, where everyone concerned expects to change. The businessman must allay his employees' doubts and remember that a risk taken in a few months by management and even accepted by the public may not be accepted by some employees for years, and by then other risks, other changes, may be under way.

Risks of esteem are never really completed. Once when Geraldine Farrar, the great soprano, met Enrico Caruso backstage before a performance, she found the tenor tortured, pacing anxiously. "You, the great Caruso, afraid?" she asked incredulously. "Why are you afraid? Surely no one in the world is better."

"Of course," Caruso replied. "You can go out and give one hundred percent, but people expect Caruso to give one hundred and fifty percent."

Once you have made a reputation for yourself and have become what you sought to be, you know how far you can fall when you fail. People who win great esteem also create expectations in others that they will continue to succeed. People commonly expect that a person's fame and glory must be matched or surpassed. As one tries harder and becomes better at what he excels in, his joy in performing increases and should nurture him. His satisfaction is in doing what he loves, and his accomplishment is for himself. The search for esteem should eventually become internalized as a search for one's best, and the attempt to impress others becomes replaced by the desire to please one's self.

The passing situation is largely the creation of each driver. In it he finds the conflicts, the ambivalence and the lack of resolve that attend his actions in everyday life. All risking follows the model of passing, although the critical variables—knowing what issue is most important, understanding what may be lost and what must be overcome—change with each risk. But the process—the sense of rapidly changing landmarks, the fear of the unknown, the initiation of the leap, the possible interference of others, the potential for self-defeat and the need for a belief in a longer journey worth taking a risk for—is shared by all.

4

Evaluating Your Risk

The hardest task is to evaluate your own needs and life and make a decision to risk or not that is in your best interests. No one can evaluate your risks but you, but whenever you look at yourself your vision is impaired, your logic subverted and your honesty undermined by your fears and hopes. Many of the questions that need to be asked before, during and after risking simply do not occur to people when they are caught up in the excitement and confusion that accompany taking a chance. The following questions are specifically designed to cut through this disorganization and help you find your own way.

To get the most out of this section, ask yourself each question aloud in private, giving the most honest and complete answer you can before moving on. You will find that the questions are designed to open up your thinking. Even if a question seems repetitive, take time to answer it, because the context of each question is different. The object of this approach is to help you break through some of the bonds that now keep you from seeing your risk clearly, approaching it decisively and following it through successfully.

PREPARING TO RISK

Is this risk necessary?
Can I reach my goal in another way?
Is the potential loss greater than the possible gain?
What can I lose by taking this risk?
How will I know I am losing this?
What can I do to prevent these losses from occurring?
What do I need to know before taking this risk?
Why don't I know it?
Who can tell me what I need to know?
Who else should know about this risk? Why?

What would be the perfect time to act?
Will that time ever come?
What makes risking necessary now?
What would be the worst time to act?
Who wants me to succeed at this risk?
Who secretly wants me to fail at this risk?
What part should I let these people play in my life?
Who else can profit by this risk?
Who else can lose by this risk?

What feeling am I trying to express in taking this risk?
Will people think better or worse of me if I succeed?
Do I care?

Do I want people to have a certain opinion of me? What is it?
Whose attention would I like to get?
Why can't I just talk to them and tell them?

Am I ever a little irrational?
Is this one of those times?
How do I know?
What can I do about it?

Am I afraid?
Of what (if yes)?
Why not (if no)?
Am I ready to act?
Will I ever be ready to act?
What is holding me back?
When will I have risked more than I can afford to lose?
How can I hurt the following people in taking this risk?
  —myself
  —my spouse
  —my kids
  —my parents
  —my friends
  —my associates
In what order of priority do I place them?
How much can change because of this risk?
If I am taking more than one risk, which one is the most important? Why?

Is anyone pressuring me to do this?
What would make me change my mind about taking this risk?

Am I doing this to please someone else?
Have I told that person I feel this way?
Have I ever taken this risk before?
Could I have taken it more safely earlier?
Why did I postpone it then?

QUESTIONS TO ASK BEFORE GETTING INVOLVED WITH ANOTHER PERSON

What will happen if I commit myself to the other person?
Does the other person understand our relationship and commitment in the same way I do?
What do I want from the other person?
Can the other person give me that?
Have I ever been close to anyone else? What is different now?
Why are events becoming urgent now?

How do I know I am serious about my feelings?
How do I know the other person is serious about his?
How much do I care about the other person's feelings?
How much does he care about mine?
Can I trust the other person?
Does the other person trust me?
What could go wrong between us?

What do I like least about the other person?
Does the other person know that?
What would I not share with the other person?
Do I need the other person to be complete?

Do I feel complete by myself?

Am I free to say no?

Do I have to give up something or change in order to love the other person?

What doesn't the other person know about me that would hurt me/him?

What would make me give up the other person and vice versa?

What do I expect of the other person?

What does he expect of me?

What is more important to me than this relationship?

Can I be myself and still be loved in this relationship?

QUESTIONS TO ASK BEFORE LETTING GO OF YOUR CONTROLS

What would happen if I stopped trying to control my feelings?

How do I know?

Who would notice?

What would that change?

What in my life is presently not in control?

How does that make me feel?

Who has even a little control over me?

How did they get it?

Can I become free?

Does being free frighten me? How?

Besides the obvious, what things in my life can I not control?

QUESTIONS TO ASK BEFORE BUYING A HOUSE

Can I really afford this?
Am I trying to impress people? Who?
Do I need this many rooms, this much lawn?
How much could I sell this for tomorrow?
Could I sell it tomorrow?
What repairs does this place need now, this year?
How do I know?

QUESTIONS TO ASK BEFORE STARTING A BUSINESS

Is there a need for this product or service? How do I know?
How much have I overstated my case to build my courage?
Who is my competition? How have they done? What are their mistakes?
What are my product's weak points? Can they be fixed?
How much debt can I comfortably afford?
When should I go into debt?
What can I not postpone?
Whom am I trying to sell to? Do they need and can they afford my product?
Where, when, how, is the best way to sell my product? Why?
Should I start a company to manufacture this

product or should I license someone already established to make it?

Who will steal my idea?

QUESTIONS TO HELP EVALUATE YOUR CAREER RISKS

Who is the most important person I have contact with?

Can I please him and still move ahead?

What concerns do the people around me have about my work?

Who is most threatened by me at work? Why?

How can I avoid making others fearful, defensive and therefore against me?

Where is the person who last held my position? Why did he leave?

Can I get what I need here?

Who has the power to say no to me?

What will make him say yes?

Why am I with this company?

Where do I want to be next year, in five years, in ten years?

Am I doing my best work?

Am I happy doing my work?

Do I need a change?

RISKING MONEY

Money risks are not always what they seem to be. When you risk with borrowed money, you are risking other people's trust in you. You are testing your worth, your ability to repay, the good other people credit you with. A risk of borrowed money is a risk of worthiness. Attempts to collect borrowed money are called repossession and attachment, indicating the dependent nature of the relationship between the borrower and the creditor.

A risk of your own money is a risk of your own power base and your ability to be in control.

A risk of investors' money, is a risk of your esteem, your reputation.

Because money risks are not all alike the questions one must ask before taking them are different.

QUESTIONS TO ASK BEFORE BORROWING MONEY

Do I want to feel indebted or attached to another person?
Will I be able to pay this back?
What would happen if I couldn't pay this back?
How will I feel if others have control over me?
Am I afraid of being on my own?

QUESTIONS TO ASK BEFORE INVESTING YOUR OWN MONEY

How would I feel if I lost it all, besides sad?
What am I getting for my investment besides a sense of power in making it?
Is there any way I could get this feeling without investing?
If I am investing with someone else, why did they come to me?

How did the other person know I had money?
Was anyone else willing to invest besides me?
How much control over my own money will I
have?
Can I act to protect my investment or will some-
one else have that power?
How will I know how my investment is doing?
Can I trust the other people involved in this ven-
ture? How much?
Do I need a lawyer?

QUESTIONS TO ASK BEFORE
INVESTING OTHER PEOPLE'S MONEY

What do other people expect of me?
Have I oversold my optimism to get investors
interested?
Will I disappoint them with even modest success?
Would I be willing to put my own money in this
venture?
Am I willing to take greater chances with other
people's money than with my own?
Am I willing to be completely open with others
about their money?
How badly do I need to feel like an entrepre-
neur?

QUESTIONS TO ASK BEFORE RISKING
YOUR REPUTATION

Am I willing to try my best?
What am I most afraid other people will see in
me?

Who really knows me best?
Do I like him?
What embarrasses me the most?
What would happen if I failed?
What would I really call success?
How much applause do I need?
Whose applause do I need most?
Toward whom do I feel most competitive?
Whom do I really want to impress? How? Why?
Who or what impresses me the most?
What would damage my reputation the most?
What would add to my reputation the most?
How important is other people's opinion of me?
Why?
Who knows me as I really am?

QUESTIONS TO ASK BEFORE GOING ANY FURTHER

When should I give up?
Will this risk really make me happy if it's successful?
How do I know?
What else will make me happy?
Do I need to risk for that?
Do I allow myself to feel hurt, sad, angry or anxious or joyous?
Do I deserve better than I am getting?
Should I be giving other people more?
Do I withhold my love, my feelings, myself?
Are other people angry with me? Why?
Am I aware of my moods and how they influence my actions?
Do I recognize my feelings?

COMMITTING

Making a commitment is the single most difficult act in risking. It is the moment when a person declares his intention, signs the contract or puts himself in the spotlight. If he changes his mind, everyone else will know. Committing to a risk is changing the matter from a private to a public concern. Others should be told of your risk only as they need to know.

Committing to action makes all the difference in the world. You are inviting other people to view your ideal and to watch you pursue it. Your honesty in evaluating your preparations is crucial.

QUESTIONS TO ASK BEFORE COMMITTING TO ANY RISK

What would happen if, after having made preparations, I didn't risk now?

Have my preparations been private, all within me?

Have my preparations created any impact?

Are the people who should be taking my preparations seriously?

Can I turn back?

When is the last time I can turn back?

Will things be the same as before if I turn back? What will have changed?

Do I take responsibility for the way I see the world?

How sure am I that events will turn out the way I expect?

What other preparations do I have to make?
Is there something I still need to know?
Are there blind spots in my vision which can do
me in?
What do I think is most likely to do me in now?
How much am I willing to bet I am right?

What is the next step?
What would happen if I didn't take it?
Will it ever be any easier?
Am I ready?

QUESTIONS TO ASK BEFORE MAKING A COMMITMENT TO ANOTHER PERSON

Am I for myself?
How much?
What about the part that is not for me?
Who is it for, if not for me?
What do I like better than myself if it is not good
for me?
Why is that not crazy?

Does my decision give me joy?
How can joy be bad?
Do I have a right to be whatever I am?
Can I ever be anything else?
Can I act in my own best interests?
What will happen to me if I don't?
Is that what is already happening?
When should that situation be changed?
How much does the other person know?
What have they said that reveals this?

What else could they have had in mind?
Will the other person follow through?
How do I know?
Is the likelihood of my backing out greater than his?
Does the other person know exactly how I feel and vice versa?

QUESTIONS TO ASK BEFORE MAKING A BUSINESS COMMITMENT

If I did not take this risk, what would I be doing?
How have my preparations gone?
Did I accomplish my goal?
Do I have a different goal now than the goal I previously had? What changed and why?
How costly have my preparations been?
Did these costs differ from my expectations? Why?
Am I trying to prove something about myself? What is that?
Who is responsible for whatever failure occurs?
Who are the key people involved in this risk?
Do I trust their judgment, honesty, openness and willingness to report problems?
Will the going be rough? When, where and why, and is everyone who should know aware of this?
Will I be limited in my freedom to defend my interests?
Who is most likely to interfere with my plans?
How can I prevent this?
Do I have a timetable?
Do I have conditions for taking each step?

QUESTIONS TO ASK BEFORE PUTTING YOUR REPUTATION ON THE LINE

Will I ever be completely prepared?
Have I made my best effort to this point?
Why not? What am I holding back?
How can I rehearse what could happen?
Am I in the right role for me?
How does it feel?
Am I competing with anyone?
Who is watching?
Why is that important to me?
What do they see?
What do I hope they will see?
Is that real?

COMPLETING

Few risks are completed so finally that there is nothing left to do afterward. In fact most important risks merely open the way to other risks. If you take the right risk, the risk that most encourages your growth and fulfillment, more risks will follow, but they will be less threatening to you. First you must get on the right road.

Accept the possibility that you may have made a mistake and try to be aware of any evidence that suggests this, without getting defensive or disregarding it simply because it does not agree with your plans.

You still have to protect your rights. You still have to be sure that what needs to be done gets done. You still need to give your best effort. In short, after you commit, the work begins.

QUESTIONS TO ASK AFTER MAKING A COMMITMENT TO ANOTHER PERSON

Am I being as honest as I can?
What am I holding back and why?
Can it ever be expressed?
What would happen if the other person left?
Am I afraid of being myself or of being alone?
Do I stand up for my rights?
Do I give without trying to possess?
Do I accept in a way that makes the other person glad he gave?
Can I ask for help?

QUESTIONS TO ASK TO COMPLETE A BUSINESS RISK

Do I know everything I need to know to protect my interests?
Are the reins too tight or too loose?
Could I have done it more simply?
Where am I headed now?
Who was most helpful to me?
How can I strengthen that relationship?
Who let me down? Does he know?
What can I learn from my mistakes?

COMPLETING A RISK OF REPUTATION

Again, risks of esteem are really risks of exposing your humanness, such as the risk the artist takes in trying to share what is most real in himself. They are the risks we take in simply being ourselves. Characteristically, such risks are more like performances, examinations, or deadlines, and they are completed rather quickly.

> Is it really over?
> How much did I fall short?
> Did I give my best? Am I proud of my effort?
> Can I still grow, improve, learn?
> What is my next project?

It may be difficult for you to understand how these seemingly diverse questions fit together. They are some of the questions you'll need to ask in order to begin to understand your feelings and thoughts and to shape your goals. It is an incomplete list with gaps, but it should be helpful in provoking other questions as you prepare to take risks.

If you take risks without asking questions, you are only inviting trouble.

5

Emotional Risks

The most important risk you can take is to be honest in expressing your feelings. If you do not express what you feel, you are forced to use defenses to keep unwanted feelings away. Whether you deny the feeling, justify it intellectually or pretend that it is unimportant, it is all the same. To the extent you do not experience your feelings, you do not experience the real world. Instead, the world you see becomes a creature created out of your needs, and your needs remain the product of feelings that have not been fulfilled.

A defense is a lie built into your character. Defenses rob you of your energy and transform you into an artificial person who does only what he thinks is acceptable, because he feels uncomfortable being himself. Feelings are the source of your creativity and energy; inhibiting their expression limits your growth.

If you do not risk expressing your feelings directly, other risks will be burdened by them. You may end up pursuing the wrong goal out of anger, or you may discover you can't act without guilt. Further, if you are not honest in expressing your feelings, reaching other goals will not make you happy.

Feelings always follow a predictable unvarying pattern:

> *When a loss threatens, you feel anxious.*
> *When a loss occurs, you feel hurt.*
> *When hurt is held back it becomes anger.*
> *When anger is held back, it creates guilt.*
> *When guilt is unrelieved, depression occurs.*

If you take care of your fear, hurt and anger, the guilt and depression will take care of themselves.

TO RISK ADMITTING FEAR

Fear is the threat of a loss or an injury. It may be a real loss, one now about to take place, or an imaginary loss or recollection of a past loss that is brought to mind by something in the present and accompanied by the unsettling feeling that the old loss is about to take place again. Old losses that have not been fully grieved, hurts that have not been settled, tend to recur in this way. A person becomes afraid of giving up the part of a loss he is still holding on to. For example, a mother who had not completely given up her dead child became anxious each year at the approach of her child's birthday and anticipated and experienced it as a new loss. When the child's death was finally accepted, the approaching birthdays were much less threatening.

COVERING FEAR

The risk people take in admitting fear varies. Some people try to pretend they are not afraid because they do not want people to think of them as unmanly, immature, weak or out of control. Still other people are uncomfortable admitting fear because they cannot accept their own vulnerability or tolerate feeling helpless.

Generally, the weaker you feel, the more you try to cover your fears. Sometimes people will not admit they are afraid because they do not want to know what is frightening them, believing that they will be overwhelmed if they ever find out. Of course, you really never know what you are afraid of losing until you look. A vague, unnamed fear is usually more troublesome to manage than a fear that is understood. The unknown carries a fear all its own. It allows you to imagine the worst.

Some people mistakenly believe that if they are really strong they should *never* be afraid. This belief is difficult to maintain, for it suggests that such a person is not vulnerable, which is the same thing as saying he is not human. People who act fearless are simply afraid to be afraid.

How Fear Works

Like all emotions, fear has a purpose. It alerts you to take action to protect yourself from a threatening loss. The body sends hormones into the blood causing one's heart rate and alertness to increase. You get ready to run for safety or to combat the forces that threaten you. The purpose of fear is to make you as aware as possible of the dangers that exist in any risk and to prepare you to meet them. When you don't admit fear, you are forced to underestimate the forces that threaten you and this puts you in the worst possible position.

Nothing is so overwhelming as discovering you are overwhelmed when you are pretending to be fearless.

There is danger in every risk. To pretend that no risk

exists, that there is nothing to be afraid of, is to abandon caution and to set yourself up for being taken by surprise by the part of reality that can do you the most harm.

ADMITTING FEAR

What happens when you admit that you are afraid? Will people really think less of you? The people who do put you down for being afraid are really telling you as much about themselves as they are about you. People who are afraid to admit fear often feel compelled to point out the foolishness of others' being afraid. The only folly here is thinking that any feeling is foolish. All feelings come from some definite event, even if that event cannot be clearly defined or located in time.

Understanding feelings, even fear, is strength.

There is fear in every risk honestly taken. If you are risking, you are in a dangerous situation, where something you value is in jeopardy—your life, your loved ones, your possessions, ideas or relationships. If you do not feel fear, it means either that you don't care whether you lose what you have at risk or that you don't believe you are in danger.

Sometimes people live in constant fear of a loss and manage to accommodate to it, such as those who live on the slopes of an active volcano. They go about their daily tasks apparently ignoring danger, but any unexplained rumble or noise immediately pushes their dormant fears to the surface. These people never really forget their fear but convert it to a higher index of suspicion, to a state of increased alertness.

When a person is in danger and cannot admit his fear, he runs the greatest risk. He may discover the danger too late to protect himself adequately or to give warning to others.

To take risks successfully you must become aware of and familiar with your own experience of fear. Just as the driver passing a car must anticipate his fear of high speeds and expect to feel afraid as he passes, you must know how much you value what you risk losing so you too will not suddenly become aware of your potential loss and panic unnecessarily. Also, being aware of the hormonal changes caused by anxiety—a racing heart rate, for instance—will keep you from misinterpreting your physical feelings and becoming even more anxious.

COPING WITH FEAR

One way to cope with fear is to imagine what would happen in the worst case.

> What are you afraid of losing?
> What would you do if the bottom fell out, if the worst happened?
> What are the chances of the worst's taking place?
> How do you know?
> How can you limit your loss?
> Can you get out of the risk before the worst happens?

If you cannot get out of a risk once it is under way and the losses are so great that they paralyze you just to think about them, you are describing a risk you probably shouldn't take.

TO RISK ADMITTING HURT

People avoid admitting they have been hurt because they want neither to admit nor to expose their vulnerability. There is a mistaken belief in our culture, especially among men, that if one is to be strong one cannot concede hurt or fear. It is no big deal to act strong because you really are invincible, rich or powerful. That's easy. Real strength is being able to admit one's weakness honestly, to say that one is hurt and afraid and still take a forceful stand and carry on. Real strength comes from accepting your vulnerability.

Admitting hurt to others can create problems as well as solve them. If you tell some people that they hurt you, they may feel attacked and act hurt themselves. If someone hurts you, it is your emotional obligation to express your hurt in a direct way, to make the other person aware of your feelings. If the other person continues to hurt your feelings after you have told him, then you know he doesn't really care about you, because you *are* your feelings.

If the other person denies he hurt you, you have your hurt feelings to testify to the fact that he is wrong. You know what you feel. Telling another person he hurt you is a confrontation between your reality and his. Once you tell the other person how you feel, stand back and observe how he deals with the truth you have presented. Perhaps in no other moment of personal interaction do events become as clear as this. Does he listen, try to ignore what you say, act in a patronizing way, belittle you or try to make light of your hurt? At this moment you will see how honest the other person is. How aware, how feeling, how caring. Merely state that you are hurt. If the other person rejects you, what have you really lost? You have lost your belief that the other person was your friend. How can someone be a friend if he doesn't care about your feelings? The sooner you know who your friends are, the better. You are ahead when you discover the truth, no matter how much it hurts.

WHERE DO YOU STAND?

The risk in expressing hurt is that it puts the feelings of a relationship on the line. You are asking to know where you stand, asking whether your feelings matter to the other person or not. If you discover they do matter you have gained the knowledge that someone cares about you. When you tell the other person that you have been hurt, you are also exposing your vulnerability to him and are telling him exactly where he can hurt you. Once you have done so, you make the burden the other person's concern. You also make it difficult to ignore future injury, for now if he hurts you again you cannot rationalize that he did so in ignorance or out of a misunderstanding. He knew what would hurt you because you told him. If he now hurts you, it is intentional, an act of anger, and you have to deal with it as such.

The risk of admitting hurt becomes the risk of testing the trust in a relationship, of discovering what two people really feel about each other. What happens if you do not admit it when you are hurt? Where does hurt go when it is unexpressed? It becomes anger.

UNDERSTANDING YOUR HURT

> Who hurt you?
> Why did it happen?

Could you have prevented it in any way?
Did you tell the other person when it happened?
Will it happen again?
Whose fault will it be if it does?

Some people get angry without ever feeling or expressing the hurt that started it. Telling a person who has hurt you that you are hurt is crucial to your emotional well-being. It keeps a relationship alive by allowing your hurt to become the problem of the person who caused it, instead of making you angry and defensive.

TO RISK EXPRESSING ANGER

No one likes to get angry. Indeed, for some people getting even a little angry seems to be a disorganizing process. They fear that letting a little anger into their lives will destroy them. In fact by the way they live their lives, bottling up their anger, holding it back, they make the angry disruption they most fear come true. The anger just builds up and leaks out everywhere, out of their control.

WHAT ANGER MEANS

The reason people try to ignore getting angry is that they do not understand what anger means or do not know how to express it. They fear that feeling or expressing anger means that they are bad and that other people will think ill of them.

Anger is simply the natural result of being hurt, being injured, let down, disappointed, tricked, being made a fool of, being taken advantage of, being used, insulted, ridiculed and subjected to a thousand other injuries everyone has experienced. Anger that is not expressed must be held in by defenses, diverting you, making emotional detours, robbing you of your drive. If you hold anger in it builds. If you hold anger in all of the time it can destroy you.

EXPRESSING ANGER

Again, the best way to express anger is to tell the person who hurt you that he did so. Do it simply and directly and state that you feel angry. Just saying that as soon as possible after you are aware of your feelings will make you feel better than you can now imagine. You don't have to blow up, pound the table, shout or scream. Just say you are angry because you have been hurt and then wait for the other person to respond.

Most of what can go wrong in one's emotional life happens somewhere between being hurt and expressing the anger over it. If everyone could learn to say "I am hurt" when they felt hurt and "I am angry" when they felt angry, people would be much better off and healthier, society would be freer and more open and many misplaced feelings of anger that seem to obscure the meaning of the events in our lives would be settled right where they belong, at the hurt that caused them. Life would seem much clearer. If we were aware of our feelings and expressed them as they occur naturally, as a matter of course, life would also be much more calm. Feelings held in are the ones that create tension. Trying to present a dishonest emotional facade requires a great deal of energy. It is always a losing proposition. You can't trust someone you can't get angry at. You can't love someone you can't trust. If you can't get angry at someone, your relationship is phony.

COMPROMISING FEELINGS OF ANGER

In the business world especially, there are situations where expressing anger is difficult. Ben was a hardware salesman who had a heart problem. When a customer demanded that Ben personally pick up some small-size painters' hats that Ben had included free with an order and bring another size, Ben felt the customer was being unreasonable. "I want you to pick these hats up," the customer demanded.

"Why don't you just throw them out?"

"It was your stupid mistake, not mine."

"But they were free. Just throw them out."

"No, you come and pick them up!"

"It's Friday afternoon. I'll bring new ones by on Monday. You people aren't working over the weekend."

"Bring them now!"

Implied in the customer's unreasonableness was the threat of ending the account. In spite of being a heart patient and feeling fatigued, Ben did not even stand up for his rights, let alone tell the customer off. "The nerve of that guy," he said to himself, swallowing his anger.

When Ben decided not to tell the customer how he felt, his heart had to take added strain. Ben did not take the risk of losing business, but instead burdened himself with pressure he could not afford to carry. The more he seethed, the more strain he created for his heart, and soon he began to develop symptoms.

If you do not take the risk of expressing your anger, you pay for it in ways that are not always within your control. Telling off the boss may not always be possible, but it is possible to point out his unreasonableness, especially if it hurts you and causes feelings that make it difficult for you to work efficiently. After all, that is what you are hired for. If the boss doesn't see it this way, then you really don't have a constructive purpose in his enterprise. If you are employed to do a specific job, but are actually hired to serve as a whipping boy, you should at least know that beforehand, accept it and not get angry over it. However, if you don't want to be your boss's emotional outlet but wish to be treated as a person and feel some self-respect, you have to do something about it.

Look at it this way. If a person doesn't love you because you get angry when he hurts you, he didn't love you before. If you are afraid of losing control by getting angry and therefore hold it in, you are only setting yourself up for the day when you can't hold it in anymore.

What is the sense of living a life guarding your feelings and destroying yourself in the process? What is a relationship worth in which you cannot express what you feel? You have to risk being true to your feelings or you can never be true to yourself.

6

Risks of Growth

Growing up is not easy for anyone. Abandoning a childish position is always fearful for people who are insecure, who feel they must be perfect or who do not know how to accept their human mistakes without feeling guilty or inadequate.

Continually giving up views that no longer seem true, accepting one's shortcomings, and growing to fill the gap between what one has been and what one wants to become are the essence of growing.

Every risk is defined by the needs and fears of the person taking it. No one can tell you how difficult or how easy a particular risk should be for you. Each person is different and reflects a widely varying interplay of needs, attitudes and defenses. And so each person must find his own way. It is clear that a person seeking his place or the truth in the world outside must begin his search somewhere in the world within.

TO RISK BEING INTROSPECTIVE

It is important to share, to be intimate and to be open, but, without your taking time to be alone with yourself, the greatest growth, the deepest realizations, will not come.

To be alone for some part of the day, week or year is important to growth. When you are alone you can listen better to your thoughts and feelings and consider matters that might not surface in another person's presence. Your defenses are up when others are around, more with some people than with others. You can't trust everyone. Also, if the person you're talking to is afraid of a certain topic, like death, he can sense when the conversation starts to go in that direction and will tend to lead you away, by changing the subject or by acting anxious, or will make you reticent by doing something else equally inhibiting. Most of the time we are not even aware of the process of being inhibited by others, let alone of what idea is specifically being pushed away from our awareness.

You need to be alone so you can see yourself without the interference of others. Only then can you get a clear picture of your faults and shortcomings. You will never be able to take the risk of exposure to others unless you can first be open to yourself, although some people prefer to be alone to hide.

UNDERSTANDING YOURSELF

True introspection is both self-critical and self-accepting. You seek to understand your actions and to find the origins of your feelings and attitudes.

You need to understand the events in your life. You need to know the role you play in your own difficulties. Unless you know how you stand in your own way, your best self will elude you.

The fear of being introspective is the dread of finding a part of yourself you do not or cannot value or a feeling or a memory that pains you. You're afraid you'll see parts of yourself that you wish to disown—imperfections, limitations, handicaps and illogical pieces of reasoning. And so you will, but you can never be the true master of what is unknown to you until you make it known, and emotional pain will not go away until it is fully experienced. Besides, there are also many good points hidden by your defenses.

All you can be is what you are.
All you own is what you experience.
All you are is what you are aware of.
To live in ignorance of yourself is to be
　incomplete.
You cannot take strength from the good
　parts of yourself you do not know.
If you want to see the world most clearly
　turn your eye inward before you look
　about.

TO RISK BEING YOURSELF

No other risk is so fearful to approach as simply being yourself. No other risk is so easy to maintain once it has been risked.

People who are afraid of being themselves really don't know what life is all about. They are concerned with appearances, with what other people think. They want to control other people instead of letting them be free to be whatever they are. They seek to possess others instead of to love them.

To go through life pretending to be something you are not or to feel what you don't is not being real.

To try to control other people's feelings is impossible. In time, others will simply avoid you or humor you.

To possess others is an exercise in futility.

If it is love you are seeking, you must be yourself. If you

are not yourself, whom can the other person love? Can you ever count on a love that is not generated by the real you?

What greater power can you have than the influence you project by being your most honest self.

BEING REAL

Real prestige is not built upon the false esteem you get by pretending to be something you are not. When you portray a false image and do receive recognition, that esteem has little power to console you or to make you feel good about yourself, because it is not derived from anything real, and some part of you—the part that is alone with you after the others have left—knows it and won't let you forget.

> You can only be happy as the real you.
> You can only be the real you.
> Trying to be someone else is not really
>   being alive.
> The real you is all you have.
> Whatever joy you find in life will come only
>   from being yourself.
> The rest has no lasting quality.
> It vanishes, like ground fog in the sun,
> And cannot nurture because it is without
>   substance.

TO RISK ADMITTING YOUR IMPERFECTIONS

On the face of it, to risk admitting you are not perfect may sound absurd. After all, everyone knows no one is perfect. Being human is, by definition, being flawed. Well, where is the problem?

Even though people know they are not perfect, they often believe that someone expects them always to be good, understanding, generous, warm, engaging, healthy, strong or secure. When we don't feel positive, the feeling of disappointing others adds to our unhappiness.

There is nothing that makes a difficult problem worse than believing it is wrong to have a problem to begin with. How can you fix what is wrong if some part of you is committed to being right all the time? If you cannot admit your imperfections, you cannot take full advantage of your strengths. Denying your imperfections is very draining. You realize how much of a burden pretending to be perfect is only when you finally give it up.

THE DANGERS OF COVERUP

In pretending to be perfect, you must ignore some part of the truth about yourself—namely, the plain fact that you, like everyone else, are not. Actually the time when your imperfections are most obvious is when you go into your defensive song and dance explaining why something happened, why you were not at fault when everyone knows that you just goofed. No one is a bigger fool than someone who is trying to cover up his imperfections. You are always reaching, appearing silly. Everyone else already knows what you did and that you're concealing it.

> What have you to lose by admitting you are not perfect?
> Whom will you disappoint?
> Could anyone do what you demand of yourself?
> Why must you feel like a failure for being human?

Do you believe you must be perfect?
Why do you believe such a preposterous idea?
Worse, why would you live by it?

You're not stupid. You know other people are imperfect. What keeps you from questioning your belief that you are the only perfect person in the world?

The answer is obvious and it's not such a big deal.

You cannot accept being imperfect because you thought you had to be perfect to be loved or to love yourself. If the person whose love you sought was so worthy, he would have made you feel loved for yourself, not for what you were trying to be. It is difficult to love the real you when it is hidden behind a blind need for perfection. Maybe you just wanted to love yourself but could not accept your faults. Perhaps you needed to be the best just to feel good. There is nothing wrong with seeking perfection in the arts or in a single deed. The pursuit of excellence is noble and altogether too absent in a world that overvalues being "normal." However, to hate in secret the human parts of yourself, because you fear they would show you as flawed, is to despise what other people with all their imperfections can identify with and love most. You have to learn to love yourself, imperfections and all, and stop looking for reasons to undermine your worth.

Perfect people are unhappy and lonely people.

Go on, admit you're imperfect.

Now, what else is new?

TO RISK ADMITTING BEING WRONG

People who believe they are perfect are not the only ones who have difficulty admitting they are wrong. It's a problem for everyone.

People who cannot accept their own imperfections secretly wish that others knew about these shortcomings and would accept them in spite of them. These people tend to reject others for falling short in the same way they do. Failing to admit you are wrong breeds loneliness, resentment and distrust because you have to isolate yourself to maintain your charade.

Some people fear that admitting they are wrong is a confession that they are not smart or are not qualified for their position. People who must always be in control are especially like this. They feel their whole world is threatened if they are wrong, since they believe that the correctness of their thinking holds everything together. They are more interested in being right than in being happy. And they convince themselves that being logical is more important than anything else.

Admitting you are wrong to the people you care about is one of the best ways to establish trust and understanding. Any relationship between two people, marital, business or social, is a matter of give and take. Positions maintained out of anger and weakness seem reasonable only to the person who is forced to take them, and then only because he feels he has no choice.

Admitting you are wrong is a positive step, the beginning of the search for the truth. If you waste your energy trying to prove you were right when the evidence barely supports you, and then only by stretching the facts, you decrease your mental efficiency. You appear silly to people who know the truth, and more people do than you realize. Worst of all, you are wasting time defending a lie.

You'll Feel Better

If you are wrong, admit it, get it over with and resume the business of your life. You can't go through life covering up deceptions and weaknesses and expect to change for the better. You'll have to admit you were wrong someday. Why wait in dread to be discovered? This always makes matters worse.

TO RISK ADMITTING DEFEAT

There comes a time when you have made your best effort and realize you have lost. Perhaps you weren't as prepared as you thought you were. Perhaps the obstacles were greater than you realized. Maybe you just weren't suited to the goal. Maybe you weren't being honest and, no matter how hard you tried, you were fighting yourself as much as anything else. Maybe you just weren't good enough.

If you cannot admit defeat, you risk throwing away good efforts after a hopeless cause. Your energy and resources need to be conserved, not wasted trying to prove the wrong point. Life is part luck, part talent, but mostly work and planning. There is as much strategy in becoming you as there is in running a race. Your goal should be to get on the right road for you, to find your most effective pace and maintain it.

No one's life is a string of successes, one after another. Even geniuses have their problems, or, rather, geniuses especially have their problems. Many great works were first rejected out of envy and petty competitiveness. Other great projects were abandoned out of frustration and fear. Some failed outright the first few times. Anyone who seeks his own way also seeks a new way. At best, life is trial and error, and the choice of where and when to make a stand is not always a clear one.

A failure does not necessarily mean forever. People do

change and grow, but not unless they can admit to their own defeats. You can place the blame on the rest of the world if you want, but that's not in your best interests. It's better to shoulder all the appropriate blame for your failure and retreat intact to prepare for the next battle. Admitting failure early and reorganizing your goals is often more helpful than achieving a modest success after expending all of your resources.

A small failure can sometimes point out your weaknesses much more clearly than the most honest soul searching. Often the weakness that makes your plans risky is unknown to you because it is so small its importance is overlooked. A defeat is a clear mirror that reflects flaws you cannot see by yourself.

You need some failures in order to succeed. If you go through life without meeting any failures, you are probably playing it too safe and are not challenging yourself enough to grow.

THE ARTIST'S QUEST FOR PERFECTION

Artists fail more than any other group of people. They continually try new approaches and seek ways of overcoming their weaknesses in technique and conception. The artist is committed to develop, to learn from each work and to grow into what he imagines for himself. The artist often has a poorly defined sense of what he wants to create. He may try to portray a vague sense of himself seeking to manifest what he feels inside. His interface with his art becomes the most important expression of his feelings. At his fingertips he creates a world supported entirely by his vision.

Still, much of the time the artist's work falls short of his dream. His failures are greeted only in part with sadness, but also with relief, for at least he brought something out from within. The artist can learn as much from a sincere failure, a failure reached after doing his best, as he can from a success.

A good failure for which you accept responsibility can save you a lot of trouble. Growing is as much defining what you are not as it is determining what you are.

Admitting defeat after trying your best is no disgrace, especially if it steers you in the right direction. Even if you do find what you are best suited for and plan and work hard, you will still have failures. Failures are part of the process of growth. Expect them, accept them and learn from them. When you fail you will feel worthless and overwhelmed, disappointed and ashamed, and you will have the urge to give up.

In some way you will be correct, of course. Your failure means that you have done something wrong and that you must change what you are doing. Sometimes it takes a dozen false beginnings to start a book. Beethoven rewrote his opera *Fidelio* four times, overcoming terrible failures and poor audience response. Each time he rewrote the opera it improved, till finally it became great.

If you hide from failure and try to put the blame elsewhere, you will not grow, you will not improve, your skills will not be sharpened, you will not learn what is good and what is bad, and you will be just as likely to fail the next time.

Often, the way to your brightest success is illuminated by your darkest failures. If you accept yourself and learn to give up the weaknesses that are holding you back, if you shed the attachments to things that are no longer true or do not work, you will become free to react to the world as it is and to grow into your strongest self unrestrained by your weaknesses and fears.

To begin anew is no failure.

TO RISK ASKING QUESTIONS

People who are afraid to ask questions are really afraid to appear stupid. They pretend that what they've heard or have been shown makes sense to them. They're so convinced that other people know more than they do that they don't learn to trust their own judgment or they accept as fact that much of what one sees and hears doesn't make good sense to begin with. Worse, they accept as correct statements that they do not understand or that are incorrect. They burden their minds with illogical detours and waste time defending what isn't so.

If you don't risk asking when you don't understand, there's no hope for your ever being anything but stupid. The stupidity that is born out of fear only grows and festers. The only way to break the cycle of ignorance is to ask questions about anything that doesn't make sense to you.

This suggestion could be construed as highly subversive by those who depend on others' timid compliance. If people began to question why things are the way they are, problems would be found everywhere. But too often people are willing to take the first complicated or elusive answer they are given as proof that the subject is over their heads and let it go at that, grateful that they were not questioned in return and that their ignorance was not revealed. For example, when you go to have your car repaired, ask what is wrong and get an answer that you can't follow, you naturally think it's because you are not mechanical. When your doctor tells you something that confuses you, you think the subject is too complicated for a lay person to understand. That goes double for the double-talk of lawyers. But you're wrong!

There is practically no subject in the world that cannot be explained to the average person, if the person explaining it knows his subject well. The doctor who cannot tell his patient what is wrong with him in clear, simple terms is not a good doctor. The most important single variable in a patient's treatment plan is the patient's informed co-operation. You simply cannot treat a patient adequately without it, and don't let anyone tell you differently.

IF YOU DON'T ASK

If you don't ask questions about things you don't understand, life will become increasingly difficult for you. People will assume that you know more than you do and you'll continually cover up, pretending to know more than you do. In the process you'll become more convinced of your own inadequacy and you won't learn what you need to know because you'll have less energy and confidence to invest in bettering yourself. And, what's worse, you'll feel like a phony, because you'll be a phony.

Sometimes people are afraid to ask questions because they do not want to hear the answers. But since they already suspect something is wrong, they are avoiding a problem and doing something about it. To stay in this knowing ignorance is to try and live on the line between hoping and fearing. You don't have much time to do anything, and hoping wrong is right is really being stupid.

TO RISK BEING HONEST

Without being honest there is no way to take a risk safely. How do you know if you really need what you think you do? How can you be sure you are not taking a risk just to avoid the pain of admitting you were wrong?

Perhaps you are only precipitating a crisis to avoid thinking about or dealing with something else. If you have led yourself to the present situation through dishonest reasoning, by distorting the facts and denying your responsibility, you are just as likely to repeat your past mistakes. Your losses will be compounded by your disappointment in yourself when you discover you have been misleading yourself out of fear or guilt. When you have been dishonest, the day of reckoning always catches up with you. When you are dishonest your ability to function is decreased, because you are using only part of your resources and mind, the part that agrees with your dishonesty. Since you need the whole truth to be at your best and to do what you must to solve problems, create ideas and make the wisest judgments, you will find that being dishonest makes it increasingly difficult to live.

Without honesty, reality cannot be seen clearly and one can only hope for the best. When you are dishonest, you can only approximate what is real. It is very difficult to control something when you can't look at all of it. It is difficult to make right a wrong you refuse to perceive. When you are dishonest, much of your energy is wasted in distorting the truth and in fighting yourself.

To risk being honest becomes less dangerous the more you risk. Being honest saves time and energy because you don't have to think much about how you will react or what you should say. You just tell the truth as best you can. You don't need to remember alibis. If others cannot tolerate the truth, it is not your problem; don't make it yours by altering the truth.

THE SURPRISING ADVANTAGES OF BEING HONEST

People who are honest have better memories than people who are committed to overlooking parts of the past. A block against any painful memory is rarely specific or exact. To ensure that one painful memory is blocked from recollection, other memories and information are indiscriminately inhibited by the same process, and so part of your experience cannot be used to reason or create. As a result, honest people appear brighter and more alive than people who deceive. Dishonest people may be sly, clever and even demoniacally devious, but they have no spontaneity, no joy and no humor in their mental process. Things that appear funny to us do so because they seem familiar in a new or unexpected way. A dishonest person seldom laughs openly because he does not want to expose enough of himself to allow anyone to become familiar with him.

If you are not honest with yourself, you are missing the best part of you. The honest you is easygoing, undefended, safe, self-accepting, vulnerable, human and therefore lovable.

If you do not risk being honest, your dishonesty will eventually destroy you by diverting you away from honest goals, the only ones you can reach and still feel comfortable being you. The rest are really worthless. Of what worth is a goal when once you attain it you must be on the alert lest you be discovered as a phony because you don't belong there?

HONESTY AS A WAY OF LIFE

To risk being honest with yourself about your needs and your feelings becomes easier the more you risk. At first, being honest always seems difficult, because no one likes to admit that he isn't happy or that his life isn't going the way he wants it to. There is no way to fix what is wrong in your life until you admit it. The fear that you will be unable to fix your problems also comes from being dishonest. Your sense of powerlessness is only a reflection of a mind partially disabled by being dishonest.

In the end you never lose when you risk being honest.

Without introspection your viewpoint can't be trusted. If you cannot be yourself, you cannot be anything important. Without admitting imperfections there can be no improvement in your life. Pretending you are always right makes you seem a fool. Refusing to admit defeat drains you. Failing to ask questions keeps you in ignorance. Failing to be honest makes you unreal.

There are many risks involved in becoming the best you.

7

Risks of Autonomy

Risks of autonomy are really risks of action.

You cannot act in your behalf unless you accept responsibility for yourself. Attitudes about acting on our own are rooted in childhood. While you cannot correct shortcomings in the past, you can still grow in the present and you can spare your children hurt by teaching them to be responsible for themselves.

LEARNING TO BE AUTONOMOUS: WHEN CHILDREN RISK

When children risk, it is frequently more threatening to the parents than it is to themselves. Children often pick up their parents' fears and adopt them as their own. Children assume their parents would not fear for them without good reason.

The parents' problem is to find a balance between protecting a child from danger and encouraging him to risk. The best way to teach a child about risks is by example.

Ideally a child should see his parent as a person who

knows what he wants and is not afraid to get it. When a child sees that his parent is afraid to be himself, he becomes angry and loses respect for him. More than that, he begins to doubt his own ability to succeed where his parent could not.

An unfulfilled parent often expects his children to make good for his failures. Such a parent is only halfhearted in his encouragement even when he pressures his child to succeed. When the child does succeed, he finds that his parent is not pleased, but envious and disappointed in himself.

A child should learn from his parents' example that the process of life is one of becoming, that growth is always possible, and that no one is destined to remain a failure. It is not reasonable for a parent either to expect his child to make something out of himself that the parent could not, or to ridicule a child for reaching beyond the parent's dreams.

When a parent is unwilling to see his child as a person in his own right, it is also difficult for that parent to allow his child to take risks on his own behalf. It is not possible to spare any child from being hurt. If you try to protect your child from all risks, you do not prepare him for the real world and only set him up for greater hurt later on.

Giving room to grow and setting reasonable limits remain the central concerns of being a parent. It is impossible to establish firm rules that apply in all cases, but here are some thoughts that are useful to keep in mind.

A child's sense of responsibility is more important than his age.

A child's past performance should not always be used as the reason for avoiding a risk. Remember that children are growing, and emphasizing past failures can undermine a child's confidence. To do so is useful only when a child's overconfidence threatens his well-being by denying reality or totally ignoring his mistakes.

HELPING YOUR CHILD TAKE CHANCES

A child's rights as a person should be respected as an adult respects his own. Merely because parents do not respect each other's privacy, feelings, right to choose friends or right to have their own taste and manners is no reason for them to deny those same rights to their children. A child has a right to be a person even if his parents don't feel they do.

When a child is about to take a risk, such as moving to a new neighborhood, playing a competitive sport, performing in an art form or taking an exam, he should be allowed to express his fears of failure without being belittled. His fears reflect his concern, his investment and his caring. When you try to make a child pretend that he is not afraid you tell him that his feelings are not important. If anything, you should help your child use his feelings—for example, using his fear to indicate his weakest points so he can prepare better.

When a child is ready to take a risk, he should be allowed to do as much as possible on his own. If he fails, he will be hurt whether you helped him or not. If he succeeds but thinks you were helping him, he may not be able to take courage from his own success and may not benefit as much as possible from the experience.

A child needs to know that, win or lose, his parents are still behind him and that doing his best is the most important goal. This is especially difficult for parents who overvalue winning.

A child should learn that the most important risks are those in which he learns about himself, challenges himself to his fullest capacities, defines himself and grows. A child should also learn that he often underestimates his own worth, that he is capable of achieving more than he realizes, and that feeling sorry for himself and doubting his abilities diminish his best efforts.

The purpose of learning to take risks as a child is to become an adult who can act in his own best interests.

TAKING RESPONSIBILITY

It all boils down to taking responsibility for your life. Unless you take responsibility for yourself, you really have no right to complain to anyone about anything.

You get what you give.

If you think that you don't deserve what you got, you're just deceiving yourself. Even if at first you didn't deserve the bad times, you still stayed around. You took it. If other people were treating you badly, you should have acted on it, fixed what was wrong or left.

LEARNING TO TAKE RESPONSIBILITY

Children cannot take total responsibility for their lives because they are not yet complete people. They have not yet been completely formed by experience. They have neither the knowledge nor the skill to care for themselves, to judge the danger of a situation or to act on their own behalf. A mature person knows when his concerns are being threatened and is able to protect himself. The child may know he is being hurt, but his dependent position does not encourage him to act. The child believes others are responsible for him and expects to be taken care of.

The child's point of view is: "Someone will rescue me, provide for me and care for me."

The child's belief encourages him to stick around when things are not going well and to hope that everything will work out. Thus he does not venture into the world unprepared, on his own, too soon. The pain of the moment eventually subsides, and even the severest conflicts between a child and the most irrational parent give way to moments of calm that make living tolerable if only by comparison.

Unfortunately too many children of ungiving parents come to believe in a false hope for improvement, for a closeness or a caring that can never happen. To make their hope seem more believable, they distort their relationship, pretending it was better in the past than it really was, and thus more hopeful in the future than they have a reasonable right to expect. Such children cannot risk giving up the idea that their parents care. Their blind faith is often the only encouragement these children have.

Who's Responsible for You?

Accepting responsibility begins with giving up the hope that someone else will care for you and protect you. We are largely alone in this world and always have been. While our parents may have cared for us, we still had to look out for ourselves, even if we denied it.

There is no other road to take in life but to accept responsibility. If you do not accept responsibility for your life, for every bit of your life, you place yourself in jeopardy.

You have the power and the strength to take charge of your life right now. People who don't think so usually have a vested interest in believing they can't or don't want to be their own persons because they are afraid of being responsible.

> What are you if you aren't responsible for your life?
> Who is running you?
> Who should be running you?
> What is your life worth if you don't take responsibility for it?

What does not taking responsibility for yourself and your actions mean? It could mean that you don't care, or that you don't think you are important enough. Perhaps you think your life is someone else's responsibility. But whose? Your parents aren't responsible for you now. The chances are that whatever unhappiness you felt growing up was not their responsibility either. You've been you for a long time now and you've long had the ability to say no and to act on your beliefs. As soon as you were aware something was wrong you had some responsibility for changing it.

Should your boss take responsibility for you, should your spouse or your children? If someone else takes responsibility for you, it means that you are not able to act on your own behalf or that you cannot be trusted to seek out and become what is best for you. Other people do not have an accurate view of your inner world, your plans or potential. Others can never really act for you, but only for what they think you need—in other words, for them.

Being responsible for yourself focuses your life the way danger and stress focus your attention. The risk of not taking responsibility is that of not living fully.

When you avoid responsibility by pretending a problem doesn't exist or by hoping that someone else will take over, the results are often disastrous. Things always get worse when they are going badly and left unattended. The time you first notice that something is wrong is the time you can most easily correct it. This fact is obvious, but not usable unless you have accepted responsibility for your life.

When you accept responsibility, you are saying, "This is my risk and I am in jeopardy."

THE LIMITING FACTOR

After graduating from the Wharton School of Commerce and Finance, Andrew went to work for Global Business Machines as head of their new-products division. Andrew was very bright, thorough and organized. He impressed other people with his ability to analyze a business situation, although the people who worked for him felt he lacked conviction.

Global had already done some research that suggested there was a market for a new desk-size copier, and Andrew was placed in charge of the product to determine if the new copier was worth investing in. It was a project that Andrew was well trained to manage. He knew all the steps for analyzing a business risk.

Andrew first considered the possible losses involved in a modest failure. A study showed that Global could well absorb the losses predicted. In fact, even when Andrew drew up figures for a maximum-exposure loss—the loss that would occur if everything went wrong—he found that Global could easily handle it.

Andrew investigated alternatives. He knew that if it invested in the new copier, the company would not be able to invest in other products. After all, no company has unlimited capital. Andrew examined the other prospective investments for potential losses and gains and the new copier did seem the soundest investment.

Andrew also considered the necessity of the company moving into the new area. After all, if the company was just playing around and had no real need to follow through, the chance of its coming in with more capital to correct a failing situation would be diminished, increasing the risk. But Global had a real need to develop a position in the copying market both to go along with its other products and to establish an opening in lower priced office equipment outlets. Andrew also concluded that there were no personality problems being played out among the company's top management. The choice of the copier seemed to be a company decision in keeping with its long-standing wish to capture the smaller office equipment market.

Andrew analyzed the market meticulously, studying many reports, and decided that there was a sizable market and that the competition was not threatening.

He tried to project the various responses the competition might make to the introduction of the new copier and decided that, once it was established, Global would not be hurt even by a massive attempt to capture the market by the major producers.

Andrew also concluded that he could reach the market with his present sales force and that Global's marketing and sales division could be counted on to reach the customers. In fact, they were already reaching ninety percent of them.

He also analyzed the ways of minimizing his downside risk and came up with a plan that called for the production of one thousand units in the first test run. He was confident he could sell any remaining product to mass stationery outlets should the test fail and limit his exposure considerably.

Andrew also figured out the financial cost, the projected return on the dollar invested and the reliability of the people around him, but somehow in spite of favorable responses to all his questions, he could not take the responsibility of endorsing the venture and setting the wheels of production in motion.

Andrew asked for more time to plan a series of market tests. He authorized a small production run. Salesmen were given brochures and sent into the field. Andrew's responsibility was to analyze the new test market data and to say yes or no!

Although the results pointed to an ideal investment situation, Andrew could not make a decision. He could not take the responsibility for interpreting the data and giving the go ahead to the production staff. Time passed and his hesitation became more pronounced. News of the new copier began to spread and, before he had finished the last of his evaluations, a competitive product was introduced into the market encouraged by Global's limited success. Even with limited feedback, the competitor could tell that the product would be successful.

Andrew could not make a decision because he could not take responsibility for his actions. He had always provided others with an analysis of data. He had received praise and encouragement, but someone else had always been responsible for making decisions. His qualifications had been impeccable, but no one at Global had ever thought of asking if he had ever taken any responsibility before.

The telling clues had been everywhere. Andrew had constantly taken the position that no matter how much information he had on hand it wasn't enough, and no matter how positive or copious the positive data were, he still focused on the negative results, no matter how small or seemingly unimportant they were. He had used the negative test results to excuse himself from making a responsible decision.

No matter how much skill a person has in business management or how well acquainted he is with the steps of taking a business risk, no risk is possible until a person takes responsibility for his own actions and is willing to stand by them.

The first decision Andrew had to make became so large that it overwhelmed him. His indecision grew while his sense of responsibility waned. He needed the one ingredient that Wharton could not teach nor personnel evaluate.

RESPONSIBILITY AND RISKING

You can't commit to risk unless you are willing to accept responsibility for a loss.

To accept responsibility means that you are going to do what has to be done or you are not going to do what has to be done and that whatever happens, good or bad, it's to your credit or it's your fault.

Taking responsibility saves time. You don't wonder who will help you. You know you have to help yourself. You may get other experts' opinions, but you still have to make the decision. Should you be operated on? Should you sell the stock? Should you buy a second home? Should you take a vacation? Should you change your job? All questions about your life are your responsibility.

When you delegate responsibility to another person, you are still responsible.

When you act, you are responsible for your actions, even if what results was not intended.

> You are responsible for what you say.
> You are responsible for what you are.

You are responsible for what you feel.
You are responsible for what you do.

You are not responsible for making anyone else happy.
You are not responsible for becoming what someone else wants you to be.
You are not responsible for distorting the truth to keep from hurting another person's feelings.

You are responsible when someone breaks a secret you told him, because you were a poor judge of character.
You are responsible when people use what you say to hurt you, because you should be able to tell when a person does not wish you well, and you are responsible for defending yourself.
You are responsible for the ties other people have with you, because it takes two to tango.
You are responsible for everything in your life that wouldn't be there unless you did something.

If you don't like your life style, you are responsible.
If you don't like your job, you are responsible.
If you don't like your home, you are responsible.
If you don't like your husband or wife, you are responsible.
If you don't like you, you are responsible.
If you don't like the way you are treated, you are responsible.

This last may be hard to accept, but the truth still is, was and always will be that "you get what you give." If your kids don't appreciate you and have turned out to be miserable to you, you are responsible. If you believe that sometimes some people are simply rats intending nothing but evil, it is your responsibility to identify them and get out of their way. If those rats happen to be your kids and you feel you need to be around them to get love, you are still responsible for not finding a fulfilling life of your own.

If you do not believe you are responsible, be very careful about taking risks, because you are likely to let yourself down at the very moment when you most need yourself and your best efforts.

You are responsible for everything in your life, all the successes and all the failures. Accept your successes with modesty and gratitude that your plans have worked out. Accept your failures as realities from which you must learn. If you do not accept responsibility for your life, you can brush off your failures thinking that you have nothing to learn from them. But if you accept responsibility, you have something to learn from everything and therefore you have the best chance of growing to meet the future.

Without taking responsibility for your life, you will never be happy, because no one can fix your life but you.

Without taking responsibility for your life, no risk is worth taking, since you will not feel joy at your success and living becomes an exercise in hope.

When you take responsibility for your life, you also assume responsibility for your past and thus can gain new insights from it. You don't need to make any more mistakes to profit from looking at yourself honestly and accepting what you have done. You'll feel a lot better right away and your future will be in your own hands because you recognize your role in the past.

RISKING DOING IT ON YOUR OWN

For many people, being on their own is the biggest risk in life, the one that they try to avoid. Most people try to be independent, to be free, their own person. But if you look closely at most people you'll find that some part of them is attached to something bigger and stronger. To put it simply, some part is afraid to be on its own.

Apron strings are apron strings whether they are tied to parents, one's alma mater, the family business, a relationship, a profession or a set of beliefs. People fear the loss of protection and support.

The fact is that we cling to apron strings because we fear taking care of ourselves and admitting that what stands between us and starvation or deprivation is us. We fear cutting the apron strings because we are afraid that if we fail, we will fail, and if we fall, we will fall.

BEING ON YOUR OWN

The best part about being on your own is that you are able to protect yourself without constantly worrying if the person who holds the other end of the apron strings will release his grip in displeasure and abandon you. You worry only about what you can affect, about what is important.

Should you fail, on the other hand, you have no one to blame but yourself. And you never really did. You may think that just because you may be bound by someone else's rules and procedures and are not on your own you can blame others. The fact is that you are always you and your success or failure is always in your hands. You may make more mistakes on your own but, because you are in charge, you will probably catch and correct your errors sooner. If you are paying the bill, it is unlikely that you will waste time or resources as foolishly.

Being on your own makes you more efficient by making you more real. Before you may have been taking your time, planning the day when you would leave and strike out for yourself. Once you are on your own you free your mind from reciting the repetitive, profitless, time-consuming fantasies, which you may now call being "discreetly cautious" or "seriously thinking about making a change." When you are on your own you realize how much time you wasted tugging at apron strings, judging their length, estimating the resistances you would meet by untying them and anticipating the frowns and disdainful glances you'd face. The truth is that you are already standing on your own two feet, and the strings are only as tight as you want them to be. They do not break by pulling. Pulling only invites the person on the other end to try to keep you in line. You break apron strings by cutting them, letting go and going your own way.

CUTTING THE APRON STRINGS

With the loss of apron strings people fear not being cared for. If you are sensitive to someone's love being taken away and dread the helplessness that such an event evokes, you may feel too uneasy to cut all the strings at once and you shouldn't.

On the other side there is the reward of being your own person, of being free. Freedom is without comparison. When you are free to be your own person, even a little courage grows to help you meet the demands of the world. Freedom makes you stronger. When you hold on to unneeded supports you become weakened. In time you may outgrow your need for the help of others, but you can only outgrow your belief that you must still hold on by finally letting go, doing it all by yourself and giving it everything you have.

TO RISK TRYING YOUR BEST

People are afraid of trying their best for two apparently opposite reasons. They are afraid of both failing and succeeding.

THE FEAR OF FAILING

A person who is afraid of failing may have grown up with the expectation that he will be special, perfect or extraordinary, and believes that his performance is living proof of his worth. As one tests himself in the world he encounters failure. Everyone does. But because these people are afraid that one failure proves they are worthless, they are unable to do their best and so hold a little back to save face. Ironically, the little they hold back is just what they need to succeed.

Of course, almost everyone fears failure and fears any great test of his worth. School examinations and the dread they cause are good examples of this. Few people ever reach one hundred percent of their capacity because of some fear of trying. You cannot do your best unless you like yourself and are willing to accept some realistic definition of your limitations. Even if your best work is rejected, you should still be able to feel good about being you. Unfortunately this is not always easy to remember, especially when you're having an off day, week or season.

The Fear of Success

Some people fear success, for with success comes the envy of friends and the resentment of people who are not as talented or do not try as hard. Some people dread the isolation of being better. Some people dream of an unrealistic success so much greater than they can accomplish that they would rather live with untried fantasies than settle for a lesser view of themselves. Other people fear success because they feel uncomfortable doing better than their parents or believe that in climbing to the top they must be ruthless and aggressive, qualities that repulse them or that remind them of people they dislike, whom they have encountered on the way up. Still others fear being in charge, taking responsibility or being the hated boss.

The proper goal for each person is to find himself and become a success at being whatever he is, competing with no one, learning to be himself without apology. If you do that you will find that you are not as great as you may have dreamed, but on the other hand you aren't as bad as you feared.

TO RISK DEFENDING YOUR RIGHTS

A person who does not defend himself does not believe he is worth taking a risk for. You cannot adequately defend yourself unless you love yourself. Defending yourself means standing up for your rights and for what you believe. Generally the two are related.

You have the right to be a person and to be treated like

a person. This means that your feelings are important and that your ideas deserve a hearing. Whether they are followed or not depends on their worth, but the right to air your thoughts and to be listened to is yours, providing you do not try to censor others.

To Have a Dream

You have the right to have a dream, no matter how foolish it seems to others or how unreasonable. As long as you do no one harm you have the right to pursue your dream. There is no one who can tell you that your dream is wrong—no one but you. When you ask other people for their opinion about your plans, remember that change and new, untried ideas frighten people. Don't expect encouragement. Expect others to discourage you the same way they dissuade themselves. It is very easy to put down another person's idea. Only *you* should put down your dream, and then only after you have lived with it, tried it or seen the impossibility of it. Otherwise you'll always wonder.

You have the right to exclude from your company anyone who offends you, who does not wish you well or who speaks ill of you.

You do not need to endure the presence of someone who wishes to antagonize you or ridicule you.

To Live Your Own Life

You have the right to live your own life, to create a life style that you find comfortable, and to build a life that is worth taking risks for. If you do not exercise this right, incorporating it into the way you live your life, it is difficult to see how you will ever be happy.

To Create a World of Your Own

Each person must take the risk of creating a life of his own, assembling the best parts of his past and weaving them together into a story that has the most optimistic chances in the future. When you think about it, you are the thread that holds the events of your life together. When you are gone, who will be able to say what your life was? The parts of the world that are held together by your life will never be joined the same way again. They are ever changing and you are the center, the gathering point forming your world out of fragments. You take that world around with you everywhere you go. It is you, your outlook, your being. Since you are the only one who sees all of your world, you are the only one who can defend it.

To Make Your Life the Best

You have a right and an obligation to make your world the best you can imagine. When you are unhappy your whole world is sad. You color your world with your feelings. Everywhere you go you create an emotional wake affecting the mood of the people around you. You are your world and so you have the chance to make it go your way, but only if you accept responsibility for your life.

The best defense is to create a world where you can be honest with your feelings, unguarded, open and intimate, needing only your freedom and the time to be yourself.

The rest is pretense, no matter how it appears.

BEING FREE

> To accept responsibility for everything in
>   my life,
> To see a purpose worthy of my best,
> To act on behalf of my best self,
> To be open, to be free being me.

8

Risks of Change

If you do not risk changing when the time is right, you will probably be forced to change when you are least prepared for it.

There is a time for giving up the old and moving on. The moment varies with every person. There are no set patterns or times when one grows to a new understanding. Each person is the sum of his experiences and must move at his own pace.

TO RISK CHANGING

Do not waste time hating your past or your life. No matter how bad it was or is or how much suffering you endured, it was all necessary to enable you to change, to move in the direction that is best and at the time that is right for you.

Think of it this way: if you had an opportunity to grow when you were so involved in a struggle that you couldn't get any distance or when you didn't understand your role in your problems, you probably would have ruined your chances.

WHY SUFFER NEEDLESSLY?

Sometimes one must endure a difficult, painful situation to know what to do. Before you can act, you must believe you need to change. It takes a lot of discouragement for some people to give up self-destructive attitudes. Others go through life hoping to be rescued by a magical act that will pull them up from the dregs. Although few are resurrected by external forces, the hope to be saved is common, especially when one is desperate. Giving up that hope and accepting the idea that each person is the agent of his own change and growth is arrived at differently by everyone.

LETTING GO OF WHAT'S WRONG

The time you spent suffering was not wasted if it provided a point of resolution for you. Merely being able to say, "I will never go back to that life again," can be a source of strength for maintaining a commitment to change.

Some risks are taken only in their own good time. Many hopeless marriages stay intact until one of the partners reaches a point when change is thinkable. For some this time comes when they feel the children are old enough to endure a separation and divorce, for others it comes when a new love has answered the question of their lovability, for still others it comes when they feel they have suffered enough so that they no longer feel guilty.

To be sure you are doing the right thing in changing, you must admit and understand the mistake you made in the first place. It is common to find partners rushing from one unhappy marriage into a second that will soon be unhappy in precisely the same way. This is not change, but a partner's feeble attempt to prove he was right all along.

It's Your Attitude

Change starts with a shift in attitude toward what you perceive, feel and experience. The external world is pretty much the same for everyone. It is what happens inside each of us that varies and can change the most. We change for the best by seeking a higher level of honesty in feeling and by learning to accept ourselves and others as we are, not by being blind to our faults or needs out of fear. Without this honesty there is no real change. Instead, we are forced to repeat negative experiences and distort the world just to prove we were right, just to cling to a false sense of safety.

How Can It Be Right if It Hurts So Much?

Perhaps it takes pain to make people realize the futility of their self-deceptions. Perhaps we are all really stupid when it comes to making sense of our own shortcomings. In the end it is our feeling of self-love that comes to the rescue, a statement from deep within us that whispers, "This is really terrible. Why am I doing this to myself? Why must I live my life in a loveless relationship? Why must I struggle with a demanding, thankless boss? Why do I have to be bored at my job my entire life? Why do I have to deny myself the hope of being what I want? Why do I have to go on living like this in pain? Don't I deserve better? Why must I settle for an unhappy life?"

Only when these questions are allowed to become the driving force in your life that they were intended to be, only when you can admit that you want more than you have been getting, and only when the pain of your life is allowed to settle in on you like an unwelcome guest can you gather your forces and change. How long it takes depends on you.

> No one can make you change.
> No one can stop you from changing.
> No one really knows how you must change.
> Not even you.
> Not until you start.

TO RISK BREAKING BAD HABITS

Again, people nurture bad habits simply because they do not love themselves.

Take smoking as an example. There is no question that smoking tobacco is a real threat to your health. It is not a risk, because it always does damage to your body. Whom do you dislike badly enough to wish upon them the damage that being a heavy smoker does? How can you rationalize hurting yourself in the same way? While you may not always be good to yourself, at least you shouldn't make a habit of hurting yourself.

So Why Do You Do It?

You keep a bad habit to have something to lean on: you drink too much to have the momentary illusion that the pressure is off; you overeat to feel rewarded. But drinking has only masked the pressure and overeating only depletes you. On top of it all, you feel guilty you've weakened. Bad habits sap your strength and rob your time. You know all this already, you say, and it still does you no good? The truth is that you can't give up doing something that hurts you unless you know that it hurts you and value yourself. The lack of value you feel for yourself shows in everything else you do. When your self-image improves, so does your life. Breaking bad habits that hold you down is the beginning of being free.

A bad habit is a form of self-punishment. Unfortunately, some bad habits are also addictions, more difficult to conquer and more self-punitive than originally intended.

Breaking all bad habits begins with accepting yourself as you are, admitting your failings, recognizing how hard you must try and taking the risk of feeling the pain from which you are now hiding.

TO RISK SAYING YES

Sometimes it's harder for people to give in to what they really want than to do what they hate.

Saying yes to something that gives you pleasure, that makes you feel good, requires that you think well of yourself, and believe that you are worth doing something nice for. That may seem like a simple point, but it becomes complicated, because it has a long history behind it.

WHAT ARE YOU AFRAID OF?

Saying yes to what has been prohibited by custom, upbringing, prejudice or teaching requires a great deal of courage. When something pleasurable is forbidden to a child, it's usually done with threats of punishment, and the child fears being regarded as bad or having love withdrawn. It's no wonder that some people are afraid to enjoy themselves.

If something is good and gives you pleasure, why should your parent have wanted you to avoid it? When a parent fears enjoying himself, his child grows up to feel he is doing something wrong when he seeks pleasure. He feels guilty as if seeking pleasure is an angry act directed at his parents, his religion or society, when it is really a private matter, his business entirely. Of what harm is it to do things that give you pleasure if they do not harm anyone else?

WHY PUNISH YOURSELF?

People who are self-punitive tend to be extremely self-centered and vacillate between overestimating their worth and their worthlessness. They are not able to say yes to pleasure because they do not really feel comfortable feeling good. The positive feelings they do have are often exaggerated just to make them easy to deny. When they give to themselves they do not feel they deserve it. It's easier to say no.

WORK AS AN ESCAPE

Sometimes people fear taking time off because they are afraid to give up their view of themselves as all important. An example is the hard-driving businessman who refuses to take a vacation because he dreads discovering he isn't needed. He may claim that he needs to work for the sake of the company and his family, but the truth is that he refuses to enjoy himself because his only identity and refuge is in work and he feels better denying himself. People who hold in their anger often work out the guilt it creates in this way.

A person who works all the time is avoiding the people

he is supposed to love. It is difficult to get angry with someone who is killing himself by working on your behalf. These self-denying people have a knack of becoming involved in other people's lives. They do for others what others could just as easily do for themselves. Some mothers never let their children do anything around the house, claiming that the children are not neat or will just make a bigger mess. Over the years such a mother ends up in the role of housemaid. She passively encourages other family members to take advantage of her. She is always too busy and too tired to enjoy herself or spend time with her family. She feels unappreciated and hurt when other family members complain that she has no time to talk to them. It is hard to attack someone who has been sacrificing on your behalf.

To say yes means you think you are worthwhile and important, responsible for making yourself feel good. It also implies that you don't need to control other people's feelings by making them feel guilty.

To say yes to pleasure means you are healthy.

TO RISK SAYING NO

The people who have difficulty saying no are not the same people as those who have difficulty saying yes. The person who cannot say no is usually afraid of being rejected.

SETTING LIMITS

People who fear saying no often have a poorly defined concept of themselves. They have a poor idea of their own limits and so cannot set limits for others. For them to say no they would first have to define themselves. This is one task they are unprepared for and wish to avoid. They want to remain hidden in others' good graces. To say no to these people means to be withholding and angry. Some people are afraid to say no because their parents always said no to them, and they fear being like their parents. They are paralyzed by their past anger at their parents and unable to feel free of guilt in the present.

CHILDREN SEEK LIMITS

If you do not set limits, people will walk all over you. If you do not set limits with your children, they will push you to outlandish extremes until you do. If you think it is difficult to say no to an unruly adolescent, wait ten minutes till he really gets out of control and you'll find it impossible to say anything else.

Without setting financial limits many households are brought to the point of ruin, children become spoiled, expectations begin to lose touch with what is possible, and it becomes increasingly difficult for people to be happy with what they have. It is especially difficult for the parent who feels he is a failure to say no when he believes that he should be able to give his family more.

Saying no is especially difficult for some people because they prefer to be in a dependent or passive role, not in the role of the aggressor, the role that they prefer to act against, not play.

To risk saying no is also to assert your territorial limits. Therefore to say no is to risk a fight, to risk a showdown.

It is sometimes easier to say yes, but the conflict will return as the aggressor continues to demand more, seeking to have limits defined.

LEARNING TO SAY NO

Sometimes you can find peace only by saying no.

You have a right to say no because you have a right to protect yourself, your integrity, your feelings, your possessions and your ideas. You owe it to no one to yield against your will. To yield out of fear for the moment to save yourself may sometimes be your only choice, but to yield all the time, merely to avoid a confrontation, is rarely in your best interests. Such giving in erodes your self-image and makes it more difficult for you to assert yourself in the future.

If you want to be at your best, you have to say no to anything that detracts from this best view of yourself. If you will not take the step to protect yourself and your interests, it is unlikely that anyone else can or will.

Learning to say no can be one of the most positive things you can learn to do.

Sometimes saying no is not enough, and more distance is required than limits.

TO RISK SEPARATING FROM
ANOTHER PERSON

A separation can mean many things.

A separation can mean the end of a relationship and the beginning of proceedings that lead to a divorce.

It can be the first time that the two parties have had a chance to examine their lives apart from each other and to discover what they really want and what they believe is important.

It can signify the end of preoccupation with worry over a dreaded split and the beginning of taking positive action about one's life.

A separation can also mean a time of simply getting away from each other without any attempt to solve problems—merely a time to cool off.

To separate is to help solve problems in your relationship that are now made worse by living together. There comes a time in the heat and confusion of an ingrown, crowded relationship when the best thing to do is to get distance. When the needs of one day become the problems of the next, when partners go to bed in anger and wake up finding fault with each other, each needs time and space away from the other.

WHEN A RELATIONSHIP CHANGES

When a relationship that once offered a feeling of newness and rejuvenation becomes a source of hurt and disappointment, partners try to blame each other for the loss each has suffered. The hurt gets in the way of expressing or accepting what tenderness is left. Both feel cheated and want their relationship to be as before.

Many things can happen to a relationship between two people when it goes badly but one thing is certain: it can never be like it was, even when the yearning pull of old needs leads you to feel differently.

People change and grow. Ideals that were once believed in without hesitation are now questioned openly. One partner seeks new horizons. The other becomes fearful and wishes to hold back. One partner wishes to explore his emotional life, to understand his feelings and clear himself of the emotional debts of the past. The other may not wish to look within and may view the partner's search not as a personal quest but as an abandonment or betrayal.

GROWING APART

How could you stop believing in us?
How could you stop loving what we were?
All the things we collected together,
Were they only attempts to fill the distance
        between us,
Futile exercises in sharing time?
Did we really share so little?
A passion that withered,
Expecting the same love night after night,
Did we age our love prematurely by
        expecting too much?
If we knew so little when we chose each
        other
How can we be sure if now,
With the shouting still fresh in our ears,
That we are doing the right thing by
        growing silent
And moving apart?

ADMITTING THE TRUTH

To separate is to admit that what once was, no longer is. The act of separation does not change the truth. It just acknowledges it. This is often long overdue. When partners are expected to play fixed roles in a relationship and one changes, the relationship changes too, even if the subject is never discussed.

A separation can force the partners to see themselves as persons with their own lives. This is especially threatening when one partner has been dependent on the other. A dependent person finds it easy to postpone growing when his partner is strong and willing to carry his burden. While the relationship between a protector and a dependent partner may have seemed necessary, even urgent, at the beginning, it usually changes. The strong partner soon discovers that he really wasn't so strong, but needed his partner's dependency to make him feel powerful by comparison. Both roles were taken out of weakness. As the stronger partner grows to feel more secure, his need for someone to depend on him decreases. The dependent partner discovers that he has also grown and is stronger and more self-reliant than before. Each has gained something from the other and made it his own.

SHEDDING OLD EXPECTATIONS

To separate often means the end of the relationship. When people grow in search of their best, they often find that the direction they followed when they were younger was unclear, that the ideas they believed in were not entirely true and that they wasted energy trying to support them. Perhaps they expected too much from a relationship with another person. When you hope the other person will make you complete and fulfill your needs as an individual, end your uncertainties and give you something to believe in, your expectations are unrealistic and the relationship will disappoint you. Too many relationships are begun with the belief that the partners would be able to stop searching for themselves just because they found each other. When this happens both partners rapidly lose the strength to nurture each other.

The only relationships that really work are those in which each partner is free to have his own life and sources of satisfaction from his work. Each partner needs to be fulfilled as a person in his own right. Without this the relationship becomes more important than it should be, and both partners are led to make demands of it that no relationship was ever designed to fulfill.

How to Live with Another Person

How do you live with another person? The most important thing is to find the right person. That is not easy to do especially when one is young and not really sure of himself, and therefore uncertain of whom the right person would be. The secret of a good relationship is to allow individual growth side by side with a mutual respect for each other's right to be a person, unpossessed. If you looked at your partner before you lived together and thought, *With a few changes he'd be perfect,* your relationship was already in trouble.

What must one do to live in harmony with another person? Each partner in a relationship owes the other an honest report of the reality he perceives, feels and thinks. Each partner should be free to express what he experiences without disguising his view out of fear or guilt. And yet each partner has his own need to filter out part of reality or distort it simply because some things are too painful to be dealt with directly, all at once.

Compatibility

The compatibility of two people usually reflects the compatibility of their defenses, the shields they erect to hide from pain. If two people share the same defensive pattern—for example, denying reality—they may seem to live in harmony superficially, but their relationship may not be free or may not foster growth. In fact, the opposite may be true. When two partners have the same defensive outlook, their union becomes a rigid fortress against reality. When one partner sees the light of a higher truth, or grows more open, the relationship becomes chaotic.

There must be a working balance between the defenses

of both partners so that one partner's blind spot is not covered by the other's. The power of love is greater than any other force and when partners are free to point out each other's faults and inconsistencies in a loving way, it is possible to give up old defensive patterns. Fortunately, partners who do share the same kind of defensive patterns can often see each other's faults even though they cannot see their own. If, however, one partner will not allow any criticism and the other is committed to find fault outside of himself, the relationship will rapidly deteriorate.

Compatibility is a willingness to be open even when one is wrong. It is based on trust, a love of the truth and a wish to be free and grow together.

While every relationship that runs into difficulty seems to be immersed in problems that are uniquely its own, the incompatibility that lies at the bottom of each conflict is usually confined to a few universal issues. These issues are always important for they draw people together as well as push them apart.

WHEN NEEDS AREN'T MET

Conflicts occur over the issues of openness, trust, honesty, giving, flexibility and sharing. If you need to be open about your feelings, it is unlikely that you can long survive in a relationship with a partner who is closed. A person who needs to be given to cannot live happily with a person who is withholding. A person who loves honesty cannot tolerate living with a person who is deceitful. Neither can trust live with suspiciousness, nor flexibility with rigidity.

Unfortunately life is not clear cut and most people are not one hundred percent honest, open, giving or anything else. Compatibility depends more on the intent of the partners than on where each stands in his own growth. If love is strong enough and one is patient changes do occur. If you and your partner intend to become more honest and open, even though you differ now, your relationship has a chance of succeeding. But when one partner tends toward rigidity and secretiveness, and the other toward flexibility and trust, the relationship falters. However, you cannot change the other person. You can only help him move along in the direction in which he wants to go. You do this by being a true friend, by being at your best.

Sometimes two people's energies are consumed by trying to hold together a relationship that nurtures neither of them and drains everyone who comes into contact with them. It is sometimes impossible for a partner to free himself enough within such a relationship to be able to grow or to be himself. Relationships that falter in this way often drag on long after they have ceased to be helpful to either partner. The partners lose time and miss being validated and soon begin to doubt themselves, their own lovability and worth. It is then that a separation can be the most helpful and necessary step in resuming a life of one's own.

To Separate

To separate is to take room to grow unencumbered by the other person, allowing each partner to catch up on his own. A separation is a chance to act for yourself, to regain missed opportunities and to try out your own best life. If you are constantly thinking that you would be better off alone, you should take some distance and see what it is like to be you by yourself.

If you decide not to return, you will at least have gained the strength to make this decision and to deal with the losses that inevitably follow—breaking up a home, telling the kids, dealing with lawyers—while trying to save what elements of friendship still exist between you. These are great losses and there is no point trying to diminish their impact on your life. But one thing is clear: if the separation is right and is best made permanent, then in the long run everyone will be happier.

You Can't Live a Lie Forever

An unhappy parent is a child's burden.

No child whose parents stayed together in hostility for his sake ever felt gratitude. To stay in a place where you no longer belong is destructive. Everything in your life suffers because of it: your work, your family and your sense of self-worth. When you are in a bad relationship, your unmet needs to be cared for and to be loved seek solutions that are not always appropriate. Others whom you deal with sense something needy about you and find an urgency in your activities that makes you difficult for them. When you are unhappy in your relationship you become a drain on the rest of the world.

Making Your Life Work

To separate is not the final answer, but it is a beginning. It is an admission that what has not been working is not working, and that time and distance are needed to make the next step.

Should you decide to return and work out your problems together, you will be on stronger ground. There is nothing as helpful as having some room to think clearly about yourself, without being crowded out of your thoughts by the other person's presence. A separation gives you a better idea of how much freedom you need, how much privacy and how much space. When each gets over the emotional shock of being alone he rediscovers what makes him happy. Should the partners reunite, each will know better what he is risking and will be more willing to make an effort in the areas that he now knows are really important to him.

All change is uncertain, for nothing in life is sure. Some pain is part of the natural process of growth. Difficulties arise when we try to avoid pain, especially when we construct rigid roles, defensive viewpoints or false beliefs to protect ourselves. Then we run the risk of being threatened by anything that can disprove our rationale. It is much easier to be open, admitting our shortcomings and moving on, than to waste our time and life trying to prove what everyone else knows isn't so.

9

Risks of Sharing and Closeness

Risks of sharing and closeness are taken to correct the loneliness of the human condition. Even the most open and unguarded person remains largely hidden in his being.

We live like isolated creatures, each in our own cave, sticking our heads out every so often to see who is there, deciding whether to let other people's presence filter in and become part of our reality or whether to remain apart.

We try to overcome our limitations in communicating our thoughts and feelings. We need to bridge the gaps between ourselves and others, to trust, to be open, to become intimate and sharing and to love.

TO RISK TRUSTING

To trust is to risk being hurt.

Learning to trust is the most important lesson of childhood. If you do not learn to trust you go through life never being sure of what you mean to another person, for no matter what other people tell you, you don't believe them. You hold back your feelings, keeping your guard up and your distance. If you don't learn to trust, you spend your life paying for it in isolation and loneliness.

If you trust too soon, you may be regarded as a fool who gives away too much for too little. People who have too much trust placed in them may resent it and pull away, not wanting the responsibility of having any hurt they may casually inflict upon you being regarded as betrayal.

If you trust too late you may lose everything. If you can trust another person only when you are sure of his feelings, you may undermine the very feelings you seek. The other person may resent being tested, examined, cautiously surveyed while you hold back to make certain it is all right to trust him. If you cannot trust, you will not be trusted.

You never know for sure. People change and grow. The person you trust today may not be the same person tomorrow.

If you trust in the wrong things you will always be disappointed. A person can only trust for the moment, for now. You can't trust anyone forever because no one really knows what tomorrow will bring. There is always some risk. If you trust that someone will always love you, you are being naïve. If you trust that someone will never grow away or change, you are being unrealistic. If you trust that someone will always think you are special, you don't understand human nature and are engaged in wishful thinking. The best you can hope for is to grow separately, together.

There is a difference between trusting and entrusting. Some people can be *trusted* not to hurt you but are too insensitive to understand you. You *entrust* information that is important to you only to people who are sensitive. To do otherwise is to set yourself up to be rejected.

To trust is to make another person aware of your vulnerabilities and to risk being wounded in an attempt to break down the barriers and to get close. The alternative to trusting is being alone, never being validated, never being known.

TO RISK BEING OPEN

To risk being open can be hazardous and, unlike being honest, the more open you are, the more you risk. It is one thing to be honest with yourself about your feelings and thoughts, but expressing your feelings to another person is a different matter. You have to know whom you are talking to and be sure you know what you want to accomplish by sharing.

WITH CONTROLLING PEOPLE

You should be careful about opening yourself to people who are closed, guarded, defensive and withholding. Controlling people seldom act openly. In fact, their defenses have been constructed to avoid any openness and to project onto others whatever unacceptable problems they discover in themselves. They slant the information others give them to prove that they are right and that the rest of the world is wrong. The rest they simply distort.

Trying to be open with such people can be self-destructive, for you are only arming them with ammunition against you. They will defend themselves against your criticisms by telling you that you are seeing your problems in them. Thus they not only put the blame on you, they accuse you of employing their defense mechanisms.

Although controlling people can be scrupulously honest, they can also be inhibiting and undermining, especially when threatened. Instead of getting angry with a controlling person, try to take a little distance. Set precise limits on what you will reveal or discuss. Structure what you have to say so you make your point. Tell him what you need to in a direct way, acting in control. The controlling person will hate your approach, but he will understand it instinctively and you will be getting through. Avoid being open about personal details with a rigid person unless it's absolutely necessary. A controlling person can't resist putting his two cents in your business, especially if you're taking a risk that he is dead set against.

WITH DEPENDENT PEOPLE

Dependent people frequently become attached to controlling people. They like the stability that rules provide and they often support them blindly. Being open with a dependent person is risky if you do not know what sets him off. Where a controlling person may give you irritating obstruction, a dependent person may act wounded, cling or become panicky.

Dependent people fear rejection and the loss of love. If you want to be open or critical with a dependent person, you'd better be sure he understands beforehand that you are not withdrawing your love or support.

WITH COMPETITIVE PEOPLE

People who are primarily concerned with esteem or saving face may respond to a display of openness by acting in a way they think is acceptable, rather than acting the way they feel. An example is the young woman who shrugs off her boy friend's confession that he doesn't love her anymore by saying she was about to confess the same thing, acting as if she doesn't care and never really did. Being open with a person who does not feel free to be himself is frustrating. He may become competitive under stress and use others' feelings to draw attention away from himself.

WHY BE OPEN AT ALL?

Why should you take the risk of being open if it is so dangerous and if others will distort what you say, panic, use it to control you or pretend that what you say doesn't matter? Why bother revealing the details of your life, your feelings and plans? Although you should tell personal details only to people who can be trusted to understand, the time will come when you must risk making some of your plans public.

Some people should be kept in the dark as much as possible. You should never be open with a person who wishes you no joy. You should be only partially open with difficult people, and then only to predetermined limits. Give them as little as possible to use against you. Perhaps these closed people will someday grow to the point where you can be more open with them, but don't waste time hoping, just keep the door open. The secret of risking openness is not merely knowing what to risk but with whom, and with some people, unfortunately, this means being rather tight-lipped. To do otherwise is to undermine your plans and yourself unnecessarily.

THE JOY OF BEING OPEN

There are joys in being open with the right people. To be open with people who are for you allows them to care even more. Allowing other people to know you better helps you to know yourself better. When you allow your inner world to be shared by another person it makes your reality seem more real, more tangible, something about which you feel more secure.

To be open means you share your world out of confidence, not wall it in out of fear.

It is important to be as open with your beliefs as possible. If you do not say when you dislike something or when you believe an act or a law is unfair, you become a supporter of the injustice you secretly loathe. Remaining silent over a hurt appears to others as endorsing the act that caused it.

All you have is yourself, your life, your experience of the world. To conceal your view out of fear is to undermine everyone who holds the same view. If the best people could discover the good they share and work to help each other along, real strides toward an open society and a free world would be made.

Being open is the beginning of shared courage and true friendship; it is the cornerstone of love.

TO RISK INTIMACY

To be intimate requires that you be open and honest and invite another person to share feelings together. Intimacy cannot be expected of many relationships. To have two or three intimate relationships is more than most people ever know. A person who claims to have twenty intimate friends has probably diluted his relationships so that none is particularly rewarding or threatening. You cannot expect to be intimate with another person unless you are both honest and accepting of people. If you are not honest, you will block out the parts of the other person that you cannot deal with within yourself. If you are not accepting, the other person will become guarded and will not share.

BEING SEEN

The fear preventing people from achieving intimacy is the fear of being seen as unlovable, weak or worthless. Because a truly intimate relationship is one with much feedback from the other person, the potential for being validated and finding support in a common outlook is very great. With intimacy you expose your vulnerability. If you hurt the other person, you run the risk of being hurt in return. You may be hurt merely by being so close and so committed to sharing that the other person tells you truths about yourself that you do not wish to hear.

KNOWING OTHERS

Being intimate is to be close to the truth of another person—to his view and inner world. Many people spend their lives without being intimate with anyone. For these people life is like living in a crowd where no one knows you any better than anyone else. In an intimate relationship your faults are known and you feel accepted in spite of them.

To risk intimacy with another person is to risk getting close and being rejected for your truest self. Intimacy therefore is most frightening to people who do not know themselves and who do not wish to be known.

The alternative to intimacy is yearning to be understood.

TO RISK FALLING IN LOVE

No matter how well you think you know yourself or how orderly are your plans for your life, no matter how much control you think you have over your feelings or how disciplined you think you are, when you risk falling in love you are in uncharted territory, and knowing how to take risks isn't going to help you very much.

HOLDING BACK

People fear falling in love because they fear getting close and being rejected, losing control or being hurt. And all of these things happen to one degree or another when you fall in love.

ANOTHER REALITY

Two people in love create a world that cannot be understood from the outside and can barely be described from within.

In purely descriptive terms love is a joyful madness where in the acute stage the logic seems removed from reason and other emotions are reduced to a single yearning—to be together. Lovers are capable of great idealism and of attributing wonderful, if sometimes a bit exaggerated, qualities to each other. They act as if what they imagine about the other is true and act deeply wounded when time or circumstances reveals their lover to be only mortal, flawed like them. It is always a great disappointment that fortunately heals, but unfortunately sometimes leaves scars on love's magic.

Some lovers manage to keep their feet on the ground and learn to love the honesty of their relationship and the freedom it offers them.

To fall in love is to take risks you never would have dreamed of taking if you were not in love. Your values and view of the world change. Friends wonder if you are living in another reality. But you don't care. You only care about love.

If your love is true—that is, if your love is good—it follows that it must bring goodness into your life, no matter how much upset and confusion it brings or how chaotic events become. A person who is in love is safe, full and therefore giving. A person in love is able to find hope in flowers and encouragement in trees moving in the wind.

A person in love risks falling out of love and feeling the sad comparison between his former life when everything was joy and glad bestowal to one where now no person brings happiness nor any lark consolation.

TO RISK IN A RELATIONSHIP

When two people form a relationship they must continually take risks to keep it alive. A relationship in which there is no risk is a relationship that is stagnant.

FREEDOM TO GROW

A person never stops growing. A relationship that does not allow both partners room to grow cannot survive happily. If a partner is required to remain the same for the sake of the relationship or the other's feelings he eventually feels cheated. It is an unavoidable law of life that when a person is denied the right to fulfill his potential, his ability to love begins to fade.

Just as you must find the road to your best self and follow it wherever it takes you, you must allow your partner to do the same. A relationship where the chance to do this is denied to either partner is a failure even if it never dissolves, even if other people think it's terrific.

FREEDOM TO BE

Again, for a relationship to work both partners must have all the freedom, privacy and opportunity each needs, even though this opportunity provides a chance to be unfaithful, hurtful or undermining. You cannot control your partner's feelings. You have to risk loving without possessing. To attempt to control another person's freedom and right to be himself is a prison, no matter what the walls look like.

If you want the best kind of relationship you have to risk losing it.

A person who is not free to withdraw his love is not free to give his love.

A person who is afraid of hurting you by being himself can never give his best self to you.

A person who is afraid to take risks for love never really loves at all.

Should you ever lose a love by not letting the other person be himself, the day will come when there will be no risk you would not take to bring him back, but then it may be too late.

You will take any risk to get a person who once loved you to love you again. You'll share your deepest feelings, admit your fallibility, give up your pretenses, learn to trust and allow him any freedom, but people seldom risk loving an old love again.

TO RISK BEING SEXUALLY INTIMATE

This is the era of the sexual revolution, of new sexual freedom and experimentation. People today routinely engage in sexual behavior that only a few decades ago would have been regarded as aberrant. There is nothing in any sexual act in and of itself that makes it perverse, we are told, if it gives pleasure to both parties. Perhaps that is true. The point, it seems, is badly taken and probably irrelevant to the entire question of sexual intimacy.

It is extremely rare for a relationship to be honest, open, close, sharing and trusting and not to be sexually intimate.

Our age and times have given sexuality a greater presence than it reasonably deserves. In the physical closeness of sexual acts people often confuse proximity with intimacy, penetration with acceptance, orgasm with sharing, usage with giving, sexual freedom with openness and physical excitement with affection.

Sex Isn't the Issue

Most sexual problems are not sexual in nature even when they appear sexual in form. The husband or wife who has a strong aversion to a particular sexual act may have a sexual problem, or may be angry and feel ungiving. Fears of some aspect of sex more likely have to do with one's ability to trust and to give than they have to do with anything purely sexual. And of course there are differences in taste and style.

Most sexual risks are not risks of sexual technique but risks of revealing oneself as a person and showing how much one cares. Trying to prove one's worth by one's sexual performance is rarely successful once physical closeness has passed.

CASUAL SEX

When sex is engaged in casually with people of passing acquaintance it is difficult to make the act anything more than exciting. Such excitement is largely prefabricated. It is the fantasy of people who have not yet gotten close enough to see each other's faults or best qualities. The value of such a sexual act must remain superficial with little validation for either partner.

YOU NEED SEX

Without a fulfilling sexual life, you are bound to have problems. First, you will be trying to compensate for your unfulfilled sexual needs in other areas of your life. Also, unfulfilled sexual feelings create a preoccupation with sexual ideas. Repressing sexual feelings to control them produces a duller, flatter personality.

Sexual intimacy without emotional closeness is not love. It is an attempt of two people to dissolve the interfaces between them by physical means. Even when this succeeds, the effect is only temporary. The union has nothing of substance and no matter how much pleasure such encounters bring, they are at best superficial relief, not sharing.

The deepest sexual intimacy occurs only between people who love each other. There is a vast difference between loving and making love. No matter how much you try, lovemaking without closeness is not love at all. It only appears like love to someone who does not know the difference.

When two people really love each other, there is little or no risk involved in becoming sexually intimate. What can a person in love lose by giving as much as he or she can to the other person? When love is real it gives each partner strength to overcome selfishness or old inhibiting restraints. One learns to take pleasure from giving pleasure, by putting oneself in the other person's place while they do the same. And there is no greater intimacy than that.

Even though the task of reaching and sharing with others what is within ourselves can never be accomplished completely, with total honesty or free of defenses, sharing ideas and expressing feelings seem to be our natural imperative.

As full of pitfalls as is the risk of attaining closeness, the alternative, facing the world alone, not knowing whether what you feel is real or imagined, is much more frightening. To stop seeking closeness with others, no matter how incomplete, is to stop caring about life.

10

Risks of Love

A risk of love fails when one partner cannot give of himself, when he fears getting close and cannot trust, or when he no longer sees the other as a person but as an object onto which he can project the unsolved problems of his past.

A risk of love fails when one partner cannot grow and demands that his partner stay the same.

A risk of love fails when partners are no longer special to each other.

Risks of love depend on being intimate and sharing. When the honesty between two loving people is compromised, the interfaces that were once shared between them in complete openness begin to close. Mutuality diminishes. Instead, each partner finds reasons for holding back and for not being open as easily as he once found excuses to be together.

A RISK OF LOVE THAT FAILED

Mike came up the hard way. His struggles began at the age of four when his father left home. When Mike was thirteen his mother died and he moved in with his aunt, a rigid woman who insisted that he follow each of her unreasonable rules to the letter. He did not rebel. He was pleased to have a home and contributed to the household support, at first meagerly, by working a paper route, and then more substantially in high school by working in a garage. Mike got a scholarship to the state university and eventually went on to graduate school in architecture. His ambition was to design homes for happy families, livable spaces that promoted intimacy.

Mike got a job with a small architectural firm where he felt comfortable. He met Sandy, a law student, fell in love and got married. Sandy was the first girl he had ever become involved with, and the closeness between them was a novelty to him. He could not see his relationship with Sandy clearly. He was in love with the idea of being in love and Sandy was the sort of person who could put on a convincing act of giving, playing out the idea that she and Mike were "chosen."

In truth, there were great differences between them, and they created much conflict. Mike found fault with the way Sandy kept house and managed their son Tim. If Mike had been open about his needs he would have told Sandy that he wanted to be given to, to be taken care of and to be close, but he was afraid of being abandoned and of testing his own ability to get close, and so he avoided bringing his real demands to the surface. Sandy and he fought over neatness and mothering instead. Mike also felt jealous of the attention Sandy showered on Tim. His jealousy made him uncomfortable.

Sandy knew Mike both longed for a close relationship and feared getting involved in one. Mike blamed Sandy for the distance between them. To reassure herself she could be intimate, Sandy began to have affairs with other men. When she felt more secure about herself, she left a few obvious clues that led Mike to discover her infidelity.

Bitter fighting and accusations ensued. Sandy confronted Mike: "You are the one who can't feel. I know I have what it takes." He became livid and started to beat her. She shed no tears but only smiled at him, sending him into a rage.

Sandy was as unable to give and accept love as Mike. She endured their marriage because she knew Mike was safe. Although he might yearn for closeness, he would never demand it. Sandy had many other affairs in which she portrayed the torrid, misunderstood wife and never showed her true feelings.

The battle raged for years and their son Tim began to reflect some of his parents' conflict. Tim was spoiled, effeminate and fearful. Mike found his son's problems unbearable because they pointed out his inability to provide a more loving home for Tim than the ones he had been shuffled through as a child.

To compensate for his guilt, Mike began to shower Tim with extravagances he couldn't really afford. His sacrifices made him feel better, as if he were atoning for his inadequacies, paying damages for not being a better daddy.

Tim became a ravenous opportunist, like many children in such unhappy marriages, and took everything he could get from Mike. He believed he had everything coming to him because he was unhappy, an attitude that was spurred on by Mike's guilt. Tim was not even grateful to his father, but as inflation and rising expenses eroded Mike's capacity to give, the son became hurt and rejecting.

Mike thought he had made the best of a bad situation until he met Elaine. She was unhappily married to Jerry, a prominent attorney, a man more interested in his clients than in her. Jerry saw Elaine as another of his possessions, and although he was gentle and giving to his children, he was unable to make his wife feel wanted as a woman or needed as a person.

Elaine was totally different from Sandy. She was warm, friendly, outgoing and completely without guile. Elaine wanted closeness and a relationship in which she could feel fulfilled.

She was willing to give up everything for Mike, to run the risk of being ostracized and of hurting her children. But she was not willing to do anything for herself. In fact, had she never met Mike she would have stayed in her marriage and endured the pain, probably without a complaint, risking nothing. Elaine needed someone to depend on, someone who would make her feel wanted, because she could not make a move on her own. When she finally felt sure of Mike, she began to take the slow, painful steps to break up her marriage.

Suddenly, Mike's marriage had new forces undermining it. He began to act strangely, finding reasons to be away when before he stayed home. Sandy was aware of her own evasive tactics, and Mike's activities did not go on for very long before she correctly identified them. To retaliate, Sandy became involved with an older man, proving to herself that she was still desirable and convincing herself that Mike wasn't leaving her, but that she was abandoning him.

Sandy confronted Mike with his infidelity and told him, "I'm glad you finally found someone you can express love to, because you never could be open with me. You always ran from being close." Having expressed her own as well as Mike's problem, she sent him packing and he set up an apartment of his own.

Sandy began to portray Mike to Tim as ungiving and

uncaring. Tim, more materialistic than ever, became even more demanding. Mike was unable to give as before and the son was disappointed. Sandy's new boy friend stepped in to fill the gap that his father left. Tim was easy to bribe.

Mike was hurt and angry, but felt powerless to change the situation. Sandy went on a crazed vendetta, putting down Mike in front of his son, uncontested. Mike found it unbearable to find himself in the role of his own father, leaving his son, especially the guilt it produced. He began to resent Elaine for being the force that prompted him to leave, a twisted piece of logic designed to protect himself from further deterioration of self-image.

Mike changed jobs again, to seek the fulfillment that seemed absent in his life. When the new position proved disappointing, he decided to set up his own architectural office, but discovered that recession and inflation cut deeply into business and that it was difficult to make ends meet.

Elaine finally found the courage to begin divorce proceedings, and her husband moved out. She believed she had a commitment with Mike and expected that when her divorce was complete they would move in together and eventually get married. Elaine and Mike had moments of great intensity and closeness when they were with each other, fulfilling their most unabashed fantasies.

They both believed they were in love.

As they became more involved, Mike discovered some of his old problems with Sandy now intruding in his relationship with Elaine. He began to project his inadequacies onto her. He could not be a good parent for Elaine's children because he begrudged them the relationship that he never had with Tim or with his own father. And so he began to be undermining, snide or sarcastic to them, angering Elaine.

In time his guilt also led him to be closed with Elaine.
His wish to be loved and lovable was so powerful that he
could not bear examining his own role in his previous
marriage's failure or in his new relationship's difficulties
and risk finding himself lacking.

Mike and Elaine went into therapy together to help understand, but the closer he got to accepting his role in
causing his own hurts the more he wanted to run. Almost
without warning, Mike moved away to take a position in
a distant city that promised prestige and more money,
even though he knew the distance would weaken his relationship with Elaine. She was shocked and felt that their
commitment was broken. He rationalized that he couldn't
afford to take care of Tim the way he wanted to unless he
took the new job.

The increased distance between Mike and Tim only
served, with Sandy's undermining influence, to weaken
whatever ties existed before. Mike became desperate, fly-
ing in to see Elaine on a moment's notice and making
unreasonable demands on her love that he was not able to
return. He became possessive and tyrannical, recreating
many of the same problems that split up his marriage.

The risk of making a commitment was terrifying to
Mike. Now he found himself threatened by the very point
that he had so long avoided facing. Elaine could give, but
he could not reciprocate.

Did he really want the closeness he so fiercely demanded? Was he able to share himself, not just a bit here
and there, a weekend every other week, but in a continual
day-to-day arrangement? Or was he just hot air, brazenly
claiming to want what he secretly feared the most?

The distance between Elaine and Mike provided a feeling of urgency that made their reunifications and intermit-
tent closeness rewarding, because both knew the closeness

would end Sunday night when he had to fly back. For a time the shuttle love affair worked, but soon the pain of being apart made Elaine feel she needed something to fill the time between. She did not want to sit around the house waiting for a call, being trapped when she had just gone through a divorce to be free.

Elaine told Mike that she wanted to date, for the social contacts, "just to keep from going insane at home." In some ways she felt worse off divorced than she had being married, because the social contacts of her marriage were taken away without replacement. When Mike visited he acted guilty and was so involved in his son's life that he was not fun to be with. The time Elaine and Mike spent together was a party or it was a disaster. It was the normal, easy day-to-day living that she missed. Such casual closeness and warm sharing of everyday experience comes only when two people live together.

When Elaine asked permission to date, Mike demanded she stay home, but when she asked for some kind of commitment, a time when the merry-go-round of fleeting contacts would end and a stable life together would begin, he felt pressured.

Mike could not make a firm commitment to anyone, because he could not risk being abandoned. To demonstrate that this was not so, he played the role of the abandoning person, but this filled him with guilt, creating a constant need to prove he was a good person.

Elaine could not make a commitment to another person until she could make one to herself. She left her husband not to find herself or freedom, but to find a replacement. When she decided she wanted to grow to fulfill her potential, she discovered that the very person she left her marriage for stood in her way.

Elaine began to see other men. Mike withdrew in a

rage, threw himself into his work and tried to win back his son by showering him with gifts. In time, Elaine decided that, as bad as her life had been, she would be much happier—that is, much more secure—living with her ex-husband. They began to see each other again, and Elaine remarried the same man she had divorced.

Mike felt he was cut off from everything that mattered to him. Soon he met another woman like Sandy, superficial and ungiving, but also safe. Two months after their first meeting, they were married by a justice of the peace in a ceremony in Reno. Mike had not grown since his first marriage. His brush with intimacy terrified him and so he retreated to the old and familiar where he could pretend that he had made a commitment after all and that he was right, good and giving, while Sandy and Elaine had both been wrong.

WHEN OLD NEEDS GET IN THE WAY

This case illustrates some pitfalls of taking a risk of love when needs from the past are not met and still seek inappropriate fulfillment. Mike sought to find the love he never had as a child in his relationship with Sandy. He feared getting close to another person because he really did not trust anyone, but he pretended he did. He and Sandy both depended on each other to limit the involvement between them.

It may sound paradoxical to want closeness and seek someone incapable of giving it, but Mike feared discovering he was ungiving and closed. His son sensed this and used Mike's fear and guilt to control him. Mike was so manipulated by his own needs that he was unable to be a good father to his son. Tim needed someone to say no to him, but doing so made Mike feel guilty.

You cannot place the unfulfilled demands of an old relationship on a new one and expect it to survive. The new relationship will become unreal to the extent of those demands. You have to risk feeling the losses you suffered, mourn them and give up hope for their ever being restored.

RISKING FOR YOURSELF

In a risk of love you must risk for yourself. Any risk you take must improve your chances of becoming you. A risk of love that restricts your ability to grow into your best self is no risk at all, but a self-destructive act that does not increase your freedom. Without freedom to grow into your potential your risk is not worth taking. To risk for the love of another person without risking for the love of yourself is to set up a failure in the future when your needs surface and demand to be fulfilled. These needs are to be a person in your own right, to have a life of your own and be whatever you would have been without the other person. If you do not protect your rights in taking a risk of love, you will undermine the very love for which you are risking.

A risk of love succeeds when it allows a person to grow.

A risk of love succeeds when it allows two people to share the most special parts of themselves.

A risk of love succeeds when it allows a person to accept his faults and to value himself in spite of them.

A risk of love succeeds when a person can risk everything and lose, but still believe he came out ahead because he became more open and now knows more about himself.

The highest love is the love that values truth above all

other qualities, that insists on honesty in all things and cherishes what is real, what is best.

A RISK OF LOVE THAT SUCCEEDED

Albert came from a home full of pretensions. His father wanted him to go into a profession. His mother wanted him to become an artist. He was pressured to go to a first-rate college, to take the hardest subjects and to "make something out of himself." Albert's mother wanted him to make a mark, "to leave something creative for future generations." Both goals seemed equally unrealistic to Albert who only wanted to be happy and have a good time. Father had made a success of his business, joined a country club, met people from a higher social level and strove to be accepted as "one of them." Father was ashamed of his humble beginnings and wanted Albert never to suffer the way he had. Albert's mother wanted Albert to develop some social graces. The parents attended concerts, plays and lectures trying to better themselves. Their son was an excellent student, but without goals. "With all your opportunities," his father said morosely, "I really would have made something of myself."

Albert went to college and, for want of a better idea, entered law school. He hated law school, but it pleased his father and he rationalized that he could use his legal background in business or politics or in something he liked—someday.

"Someday" never came. Albert began to keep company with a beautiful, vivacious girl, Linda, who came from a poor family. Albert's parents were stricken. "How could you throw away everything we gave you?" they complained. "This girl doesn't have any background. She's wrong for you. She'll make your whole life miserable." Albert was just getting serious with Linda. He could not understand his parents' reaction, but did not want to hurt them. He loved them and saw them as self-sacrificing and wanting the best for him. He dated Linda off and on through law school. Theirs was an intense, electric relationship. Whenever they got together, no matter how much time lapsed, the old chemistry was still there. Linda started working for a newspaper as a fashion correspondent. Their contacts faded over the years because Albert held back out of guilt. He saw loving her as hurting his parents.

After law school Albert was named clerk to a Supreme Court justice. He had been a brilliant student and his success seemed to please his father. Albert threw himself totally into the law when Linda moved away. He could not understand how Linda had made such an impression on him and he tried to forget her. In time he married Amanda, the daughter of a prominent financier, who happened to belong to his parents' country club. It was a large wedding, well covered in the local papers.

Albert had all the trappings of a successful life: an excellent job in a prestigious law firm and a wife who could fit into any life style he would choose—any opulent one, that is. His finances seemed secure. His future looked bright. Yet something was missing, and Albert had no idea what that could be.

He had been married scarcely two years when his first son was born. His second child was born a year later. When his third child arrived, he began to feel trapped in a life where in spite of remarkable success he was becoming increasingly discontented.

Albert did not find his life rewarding. In some ways Amanda turned out to be a carbon copy of his mother.

She was a student of appearances. She knew what was appropriate, what gift was fitting for what occasion, what to wear, how to carry herself, what schools were the best for her children and how to break in new domestic help. Albert appreciated her efficiency. She ran the house well, planned vacations, arranged their social calendar and was cheerful and outgoing when others were around. When they were alone together they barely spoke.

One day, while skiing in Colorado with friends, Albert returned to his friends' chalet to see how his wife was feeling; she was nursing a twisted ankle from the previous day. When he discovered his wife in bed with his friend, Albert was surprised. More than that, he was confused because he did not feel even a little hurt. He and Amanda had a long talk.

"If you expect me to apologize, I can, but I don't see where it will do any good," Amanda began. "I have needs that are going unmet, as I am sure you do, and I simply take care of those needs. Don't tell me you haven't or don't, Albert."

"No, I won't pretend anything," Albert nodded. "I have been around, as they say."

"Well, what are we supposed to do now?" Amanda asked. "I couldn't stand making any phony promises to reform. As I see it, we are exactly the way we were before this afternoon. I still want to keep our life together. It works, Albert. There's room to breathe. Let's be sensible. There's no reason to do anything differently. Most of our friends are in the same situation."

"I know," said Albert, smiling. "I know."

He went back to the office early, leaving Amanda to spend the week. He was suddenly free to do whatever he wanted, without the faintest tinge of guilt. He felt adventuresome and went to a popular dating bar just to look around. To his surprise a young woman befriended him and offered to make him a drink at her place. He accepted, feeling the need to put the scales in balance.

His new friend was encouraging and appreciative and asked for his telephone number. "Boy," said Albert, "times sure have changed!" He began to see the young woman regularly. Later, when a conflict arose over attending a party with his wife or being with his new girl friend, Amanda insisted on going to the party with a friend of her own.

Albert continued to see other women. Now he and Amanda both dated openly. Amanda was happy with their arrangement, but after a while he began to lose interest.

"There must be something wrong," he told her. "I think our dating isn't good for us. It dilutes our relationship. If there is something missing between us, why don't we try to find out what it is and work it out?"

"I know what is missing already, dear," Amanda said. "It's passion."

"Passion?"

"We're both looking for love and it just isn't in the cards that we can find it with each other. Don't feel bad. It isn't for most people. So we seek out other people and, at least in the newness of other relationships, there is the possibility of love. Come on, Albert, love is a schoolgirl's dream and we're not children anymore."

"This isn't very convincing. It sounds like a grade B movie and you should be played by Bette Davis."

"Well, what am I supposed to do, deny myself and learn to hate you for not being everything I need? Do you want to throw away a perfectly good relationship simply because we aren't in love all the time?"

Albert stared out through the small-paned Tudor windows of his den. He surveyed the antique furniture, remembering where they had bought each piece, and took inventory of the ivory figurines on the shelves—their things. He rubbed his eyes. The Fortnams would be coming by to pick them up in an hour. He had to shower and change.

Is this what I want, Albert thought, *to spend my life finding substitutes for being happy? Why can't I be happy having what I need?*

He felt hollow inside, almost cheated. He had been living out someone else's blueprint. All he had ever wanted from his parents was the reassurance that whatever he did, whatever he was, was good enough for them; but that reassurance never came because his parents were not happy being themselves.

Albert's three sons were getting bigger and Amanda was already setting their course to the right colleges. *Where has the time gone? Why weren't we close, a real family?* Wherever Albert looked he saw distance and emptiness in his life.

He went upstairs to change and turned on the television to catch the end of the evening news. The announcer was making one of his wry comments about ladies' fashions as a lead-in to a news feature. Suddenly, in the middle of the screen, Linda appeared as the correspondent covering a fashion show for the network. Albert sat back on the bed stunned and watched the segment, eyes riveted to the screen. When it was over Amanda turned off the set. "I like Yves St. Laurent better. Come on, Albert, we'll be late. What's wrong with your eyes, dear? They're tearing."

Albert was not emotionally present for others the entire evening, but no one seemed to notice. "No one notices anything about feelings here anyway," he said, half to himself. "Look at what I am becoming, I do not even recognize my own hurt anymore. I have spent so much time trying to please others, by doing my best to keep up appearances, by doing the right thing, by making the sensible compromises, by affording to live in this style, by staying here even though I do not feel loved, that I've begun to lose contact with myself. The thing that is missing in my life is me. I have acted so long trying to please the world that I have forgotten what it takes to make me happy.

"I must be a phony to be living a life like this. I don't like to admit it, but there is no way I can avoid it. I could make a case in a court of law justifying my continued insincerity staying here sacrificing for the family, the firm, for everyone, but if I spend my whole life sacrificing for others, when do I begin to live for myself?

"Never! The answer is never. I will never be free to love because I am not free to love myself."

Albert placed a long-distance call to New York the next day. Linda answered the phone and immediately recognized his voice.

Everything changed! What had been simple before became complicated and unpredictable. Their dates were totally consuming experiences, lasting hours. Old feelings that had been pushed away surfaced in both of them without hesitation. For Albert the risks were just beginning.

As far as the other people in his life were concerned, Albert was doing a selfish, cruel and unnecessary thing. "The children will suffer," Amanda told him. "They need a father."

In some ways Albert would lose terribly. Legally, his position looked dismal. He conceded the point to himself. It would be a struggle for him to maintain his assets. The courts would see him as the abandoner. He would risk that, but he could never risk feeling empty again. Not to act, not to live with Linda, had suddenly become the risk he wanted to avoid. He had made the step. He knew what he needed and what he had to do.

Albert finally told his parents that, in spite of their great show of torment at his marriage dissolving, they did not have his best interests at heart. "If you really loved me," he said, "you would only be concerned whether or not I was happy and would trust that I would take care of my children."

Albert risked not merely for the love of Linda, but for a life he yearned to live. For him, pleasing people to win their love was an act of desperation, and even when it was successful, the love it won was conditional. If the love you seek is worth having it will be given to you because you are worth loving, not because you bought it with deeds or things. The only way you can buy love is by being lovable.

People find it difficult to take risks of love because they do not feel anyone has ever loved them without reservation or conditions. They do not feel worthy.

LEARNING TO LOVE YOURSELF

How do you correct a situation like this? You can't return to your childhood and ask your parents to love you the way you needed to be loved. Each person has the lifelong goal of making himself into a person he can love. You do this by saying yes to all of the things that give you pleasure and nurture you. This is not an invitation to self-indulgence. It is a statement that says *If something gives you pleasure do it*. Buy a piano, plant a small garden, take up painting. Get your good china and silver out of the closet and use them for yourself. If you don't think you're good enough, who will? When you start loving yourself and doing the countless little acts of love for yourself that you may now think are stupid or overlook, you will start to grow full and feel cared for. Maybe you think other people should do them for you. But who should, and how could anyone know what to do if you don't show them? Furthermore, others reason that if you don't do for yourself you really don't want to be given to, and so they won't risk being rejected by giving to you and feeling your lack of appreciation for their gift.

As you fulfill and nurture yourself you will become a more giving person. Full people always are. In that full state you will feel more comfortable taking risks of love because you feel you love yourself more and because you know what is important to you. When you feel what self-love can do for you, you are more willing to love another.

If you don't love yourself, you can't love anyone. You have to make yourself complete. It is not the job of another person to fulfill you as a person. It is your responsibility to become you.

You may never find love. That is sad, going through life, loving only by approximation, investing everything in children or yourself because your relationship with your spouse is not that fulfilling and there doesn't seem to be anything in the world you find worth changing for. That is sad indeed, but sadder still is to find a love worth risking for and being unable to risk because you have deprived yourself so long you do not believe that you are worthy of love.

11

Risks of Control

Nothing is so destructive to taking a risk of control as trying to control everything. The purpose of taking a risk is to let go of the controls that bind you and act freely. People who have difficulty taking risks of control want to know the outcome beforehand. They want to have their cake and eat it too. Their attitude, more than their action, causes the failure they dread so much.

A RISK OF CONTROL THAT FAILED

Barry was twenty-two when he toured Europe his first summer after graduating from college. He had majored in business administration and had ambitions of becoming a powerful international financier and importer. Everywhere he traveled Barry looked for potential exporters of products he might distribute in the United States. To further his cause and make up for his youthful appearance, he carried business cards that read BARRY LEWIS, JR., INTERNATIONAL INVESTMENT CORPORATION, giving them to prospective exporters and explaining that his father was president of the company. In fact, his father was a modestly successful jeweler who knew nothing of Barry's plans.

Barry had a great deal of trouble during his adolescence, getting into many minor skirmishes with the law. His parents thought he was too smart for his own good. Although he had been caught in a forgery of a business document, no money was involved and no charges were pressed. Barry was always talking a big-money game. To listen to him you would think that he was the president of the Chase Manhattan Bank. He seemed overly impressed with himself, but his great personal charm and considerable good looks worked for him. He showed the initiative to make contacts, but did not have the follow-through to secure anything tangible. While many doors opened for him he only looked around, never settled down, never committed himself.

Barry was afraid of acting as himself and being judged a failure. He wanted more than anything to be a business success and he wanted to begin his career at the top, right where he thought he belonged.

At the end of his European trip Barry found himself in a café in Madrid trying to impress another tourist about "my plans and company." At the next table Carlo, a Spanish businessman, quietly eavesdropped. It did not take much eye contact before Barry and the businessman struck up a conversation.

Carlo took Barry to see his factory and observe his manufacturing process. Carlo made synthetic plastic flowers, excellent copies of the real thing. Barry immediately wove an intricate story about his "father's company" and Carlo offered him an exclusive contract for the United States. Barry quickly flew home to set up a corporation to handle the new business, explaining in a letter to Carlo that his lawyer advised him to "form a new company, for tax purposes too complicated to explain. You know how lawyers are, but you will be dealing directly with me, not with my father."

Barry showed the product to some investors who came up with substantial financial backing. Everything looked perfect. He had a superior product at a low import cost with high potential profitability. The market seemed good. There were no competitors and the buyers who saw the product were enthusiastic. Barry was in the position he had always dreamed of. He wanted to make sure everything was perfect before he placed his first order to Madrid. He did not want to risk anything going wrong.

Barry decided he needed some professional marketing and advertising advice. He had a catalogue and mailing pieces designed for prospective buyers, and he had elaborate stationery printed and billing receipts as well. Letterheads were even printed on scratch pads, "to make the best impression." He wanted every detail to be just right. He designed a beautiful office, partly to help in selling, although customers rarely came to the office, and partly to corroborate his story of being a successful businessman when Carlo visited the country.

Barry spent so much time arranging the details of his business that he had little left over for enjoying himself. He began to become bogged down in the details of marketing the product. He insisted on having nude models display the flowers in advertisements "to accentuate their naturalness," a nice touch, he thought, if a little overdone and unnecessary. He had marketing surveys conducted to determine what size flowers people were most interested in and what species, and whether people would prefer to buy the flowers in bunches or individually. He wanted to be sure.

Barry began to exhibit at trade shows and hired beautiful models to wear the flowers in their hair and talk with prospective buyers, but he was not yet ready to take an order because he was not yet sure. He studied the buyers' comments to see if there was some pattern that he could discover and upon which he could capitalize. None emerged.

Barry decided to have some elaborate packaging designed, believing that he would be able to charge a higher price if the flowers were individually packaged. The cost, he reasoned, could be absorbed by the higher profit of each sale. Of course there were no sales yet because after nearly a year of investigating the market, spending his investors' money, Barry had still not placed a single order.

At Carlo's insistence, Barry did place a sample order to test the market. When the flowers arrived, he was horrified because the flowers gave off a strong odor of vinyl chloride, a common ingredient in plastics. He did not feel he could sell a product that smelled so badly, especially with his beautiful packaging and the advertisements that emphasized their naturalness and promised they were the next best thing to real flowers. Barry insisted that the odor be corrected and flew to Madrid "on a mission of mercy," as he saw it, "to help these peons survive in the modern world."

Carlo said the odor would dissipate in a few hours if the flowers were well ventilated. When Carlo suggested that Barry's packaging only made the smell worse, Barry was indignant and insisted that the formula of the plastic be changed. He worked for weeks in the plant testing new formulas. Unfortunately, the process that successfully removed the odor also altered the color of the flowers. In the process of solving the odor problem Barry had alienated Carlo, who insisted that he place a large order and get down to the business of exporting his product.

Barry was in turmoil. In spite of his elaborate planning, events did not seem to be going the way he wanted. He had done everything right—or so he thought. His real problem was that he was so afraid of failing that he wanted the chances of failure reduced to zero. So, in spite of prodding from Carlo and increasing uneasiness on the part of his investors, Barry continued to make contacts with buyers without taking orders, and to plan advertising campaigns a year away while ignoring the demands of reality.

In time the marketplace became congested with other products, and while none were as elegant or as lifelike as Barry's, they were offered more cheaply and so found ready customers. Undaunted by his position being eroded, Barry continued to suggest additional modifications in the plastic formula and in the packaging. "The product has to be perfect," he said to Carlo who nodded silently, realizing that such a goal was impossible.

In the year and a half that Barry had the contract he investigated every possible problem that could go wrong and took elaborate steps to prevent this from happening. His energy was spread wide and thin. His marriage faltered and his wife left. Rather than deal with the feelings of loss that his divorce created, he increased his misdirected efforts to prevent a business failure. By trying to control the details of his business, Barry tried to control everything in his life and soon lost his sense of perspective. When he discovered that a packaging slip had been printed in the wrong color, he became as upset as if the entire product line had failed. He saw any possibility of being imperfect as an omen that the entire deal would fall through and as an indication that he was out of control.

Months passed, and Barry was still unable to place the order for a large shipment. Carlo sent a formal letter on the day the contract expired, notifying Barry that he would not renew his option and that their relationship was severed.

Although Barry had paid attention to all of the details, he could not commit himself to the larger goal: selling a product and making a profit. He had it all backward. His company folded. His investors sued him. His credit was ruined. His reputation and marriage were destroyed.

Barry failed because he wasted his energy, foolishly trying to limit all potential loss. Because he had looked into so many details, the more preparations he made, the less excuse he had for failing. He found himself trapped by the very efforts he made to keep from being out of control.

It is very difficult to make a leap if you are afraid that you will prove the worst about yourself. The wish to be a successful, powerful businessman occupied all of Barry's fantasy. He tied so many extra needs and wishes to his original risk that should he fail he would lose not only his company, but his self-respect, his reason for living, and his identity. He made his risk too great to take, and his fear turned him into the very failure he dreaded becoming. He became an indecisive, passive, frightened businessman who could accept no responsibility and could not learn from experience.

ALLOWING FOR SLACK

In taking a business risk, you must realize that you cannot control everything. There is no way you can make rigid, elaborate plans and expect to come out ahead without giving in or changing a little. The preparations Barry made were too complete, too detailed to be useful in making a new decision. Preparations of that sort are a defense against acting; they lock you into a previous conclusion and make changing your mind or acting flexibly seem like admitting you were wrong.

YOUR BEST ALLY

In taking a business risk, you must identify the important factors, determine what influences them most and understand what effort is needed to make events move in the desired direction: make a plan to act, and act. You should not try to perfect everything, even in theory. A business risk must be taken in the real world, not in a vacuum on the drawing board. That is why it is a risk. You have to venture something and hazard a loss. And a cold reality, honestly perceived, can be your best ally.

A successful business risk does not try to prove the worth of any of the parties involved. Companies where people fight for recognition are dismal places to work. When failures come, blame is projected onto others. When success occurs, people feel cheated for not getting enough credit. More important, when a risk needs to be taken and is justified on the facts of the case, it should not be undermined merely because the person in power feels it might reflect badly on him if it fails.

All risks of control require that one stand back and see the entire situation clearly, with the understanding that the wish to control may be a cover for personal difficulties. The overdetermined need to control a business situation will always decrease one's ability to respond quickly to a changing marketplace. And that will increase the chances of failure more than anything else.

A controlled life is one that is not really lived.

A risk of control succeeds when it allows a person to give up controls, to be himself and act freely on his feelings. People who are unable to risk giving up control live in a rigid world inhibited by "I shouldn'ts" and "I mustn'ts." They do not understand "I need to" and "I feel," and can't act to fulfill themselves.

A RISK OF CONTROL THAT SUCCEEDED

Carol married George against her parents' wishes when she was only twenty. Her parents felt that George was not good enough for her. They had imagined for Carol someone much better off financially and from a better family. They also felt that she was too young and did not know her own mind yet.

Her mother's full-time occupation was calling Carol's house to find out what her daughter was doing and to see if George was being pushed hard enough to better himself. George was an agreeable fellow, but he could never bring himself to show affection for Carol's antagonistic parents. He owned a small car dealership and prospered far beyond anything that Carol's parents had ever imagined for her. In the ten years that Carol and George were married they built a new home in the suburbs and a summer home on Nantucket.

No matter what George did, Carol's parents saw it as trivial and unimportant and compared him unfavorably to other men behind his back. This hurt Carol but she said nothing. All of her life she felt as if she had been placed on a pedestal by her parents, who professed love and claimed to want only the best for her. Yet now, when the best seemed to be working out for her, they were becoming more and more negative toward George. Although they denied it, they were jealous of George and demanded that she prove her love for them by taking their side against him. The uncertainty of Carol's allegiances began to pain her husband and make him doubt her love.

George wanted a closer relationship with Carol, but she grew less able to react to him and seemed unwilling to give. She appeared torn. He became confused. He began to lose interest in work and his dealership faltered. When car sales dropped, worry increased, and George found it difficult to cope. He sought help and was referred to group therapy where he learned, among other things, that his wife was probably trying to serve both him and her parents, when she should have been acting for herself. He began to understand why Carol had no energy left for him, and why he had to shoulder the entire emotional burden of their relationship. He resented this and felt angry at Carol's parents, whom he began to see as interfering in his marriage.

Carol became anxious when George suggested there was something wrong with her parents. She had always suspected that they did not understand her, but she was sure they loved her and meant well. She refused to express any anger or hurt toward them. That would be, in Carol's terms, like losing control, for if she expressed her feelings honestly to her parents she might lose their love. It was a trying bind and she could not act.

Meanwhile, George was becoming stronger and continued to encourage Carol to talk openly to her parents. At a family gathering Carol's mother noticed her daughter was not looking well. "What are you doing to Carol?" she asked George. "When she lived with us she was always happy, never had a care in the world. Look at the troubles you have brought on our little girl. Look at her and tell me if you think you have been best for her."

George put down his plate, making a mental note not to have anything in his hand that he might throw, and said, "Do you think anyone would have been good enough for Carol?"

"Of course."

"Who?" he demanded. "I'd like to know."

"Well, we were good enough for her before."

"And now no one is good enough? Is that it?"

"I won't allow you to talk to me like this," said the mother. "Carol, you tell him to talk to me with respect."

Carol was silent. Her father walked over to her, put his arms around her and said, "There now baby. Don't you worry. We'll help you get out of this."

"You think that's all there is to it?" shouted George. "If you get her back in your house she'd be fine?"

"Well," said Carol's mother reflectively, "yes, that's right. You're the one who ruined her."

"You can go to hell, George," shouted Carol's father. "We'll always keep our door open for you, Carol."

And they left.

George was confused and irritated with his wife for not speaking up. "What's the matter with you? Don't you have a tongue? Can't you see that they're not interested in you, only in themselves? Don't you understand that by trying to be the perfect daughter all the time and never confronting them with the hurt you feel that you're becoming a basket case?"

"What am I supposed to do, George? They are my parents and I know that they love me. I know it, the way I know my own name."

Later on in the evening Carol's parents called and began to complain about George and his lack of respect. The mother went on to say, "You know, Carol, I always took good care of you when you were a child. We always wanted you to have the best, because you were the best. I think that it's not too much to ask that you demand that

George treat us better. It's your obligation to take care of us. After all, we are not that young anymore. We don't know how much time either of us has left. Your father complains of chest pains all of the time and you know the problems I've been having with the doctors for years now. I think it is something you owe us in our later years to make life smoother. And Carol, if George is acting the way he is, it's because you've let him get out of hand."

Carol hung up the phone, confused and in tears.

"But Carol," George protested, "they always insist that it's your turn to take care of them. They always tell you what a wonderful job they did bringing you up. Was it such a wonderful job? Are you able to find contentment in life? They fed you such nonsense about your being perfect that now you can't express your angry feelings when you feel them, because you don't want to let them down by being real. Can't you see it's a sham to try and control your feelings?"

Carol was crying bitterly. "I don't want to lose my parents' love."

"You never really had loving parents," he shouted. "Parents who care would never do that to a kid."

"My mother always took care of me."

"Is that really true? I think you take care of your mother's needs. I think your parents' relationship stinks and that they live through you. You were the reason they stayed together."

"That's not true," she protested weakly.

"And if your mother loses you, then she doesn't have any feeling of justification for all her sacrificing. She should have divorced your father years ago. She couldn't really give to you, ever."

Carol reflected awhile. "You know, but it *is* all backward. I am the one who takes care of Mother. When she's upset, she comes over here and lets out her pain on me.

When I tell her something is wrong with me or express a feeling she doesn't like, she just says it's your fault and changes the subject. The only thing she ever tells me about my pain is that it isn't her fault. She tries to make my pain and suffering sound like her injury. As if she's saying, 'How dare you be upset and make me unhappy.' "

"What are you going to do about it?" asked George.

"I'm going to call her back and tell her what I feel."

George handed her the phone and sat back. "Mother," Carol began, "I have something important to tell you."

"Go ahead, dear. You sound very upset. Did George do something?"

"No . . . it's not George."

"Well, what can it be?"

"Please just listen. I think that you . . . no, let me begin again. I am very angry with you."

"What in the world would you be angry with me for? What have I ever done to you? I've never done anything . . ."

"Please listen, Mother!"

"In all these years, you never once said anything like that. Did George tell you to say that?"

"Mother. Please listen or I'll hang up. I am angry and I will say what is on my mind."

"Oh, wait! Let me get your father on the phone. Come, Richard. I don't think the girl is well."

"I am well! I am just angry!"

"What are you so angry about?" asked Father, picking up the phone.

"If the two of you would only listen."

"Don't we always listen?" Mother droned. "If you have something to say, don't you find that we listen? I don't know why George won't listen if he's such a good husband. We listen, don't we, Richard? . . . See, we listen."

"Mother, shut up."

"Did you hear that, Richard? To her own mother."

"Listen to me, listen to me," Carol screamed. "All right, now hear what I say. I can't stand it anymore. When you come to my house, you see it as an opportunity to attack George. Well from now on I don't want to hear it. It is *my* marriage. I love George and if you really love me you will respect my feelings. Your constant badgering of George and putting him down hurts me deeply. It's ten years. You think you'd accept the person I love by now."

"I only . . ."

"Be quiet, I'm not finished. The only thing you care about is you. You tell me that all you care about is me. Well if that were true, you would care about the way I feel. You don't. You only care about the way you feel, and about what you think is right for me. That may be right for you, but I am the only one who knows what's right for me."

"You're finished now?"

"No. I think we should see each other only if and when you agree to keep your nose out of my business and respect my relationship with George."

"You're telling me that George is more important than I am?" asked Carol's mother. "That's what you are saying? Okay, I have heard enough. You are no daughter of mine. Goodbye. Hang up, Richard."

Carol sat down next to George and began to shake. She had taken the first emotional risk of her life with her parents. She saw how she had been pressured into trying to accept her parents' reality in place of her own, but she could not live by their views and keep body and soul together. She had to be open with her feelings because to be silent was to confirm her parents' belief that they were right and that her views did not matter.

The next few months were trying for Carol. With the new distance she began to see just how confused and unrealistic her parents had been. More than that, she began to understand how much her own fear of being open about her feelings made her lie to them and pretend that they were right, just to avoid fighting.

In time, Carol began to feel more comfortable in giving to her family, giving without holding back or feeling that giving to George was somehow betraying her parents. The increased warmth and closeness she felt at home made more tolerable the difficult transition of establishing distance from her parents.

Carol realized that the loss she most feared, that her parents would withdraw their love, had occurred long before she took her risk. The real loss for her was admitting that her parents were never able to give their love in the first place, that losing their conditional love was neither worth feeling guilty over nor lying to prevent. She understood that to spend her life trying to secure love from unloving people was to waste her time and ruin the genuine affection that her family did offer. In fact, it was only when she was able to give up trying to control her angry feelings toward her parents and to stop withholding her affection for her husband and feeling guilty about it that she felt in control for the first time.

Carol decided to accept her feelings and let the chips fall where they might. She trusted in her own goodness, even before she was sure it would all work out. In the end she felt more comfortable simply being and feeling. Her parents never understood and never really accepted her new attitude, but they did stop badgering George. Finally, Carol began to accept their discomfort in her house as their problem and stopped worrying about making them happy. They had made themselves unhappy when they decided to be dishonest about their feelings and tried to place the responsibility for their lives on her.

Carol decided to risk being happy. If that made her

parents unhappy, their unhappiness was eloquent testimony to the insincerity of their love, and this just had to be their problem.

WHEN LOVE IS CONDITIONAL

When love is conditional on your behavior it is being used to control you. It places you in a bind from the beginning, for in order to be yourself you have to risk losing another person's love. Love used to control is cruelty, no matter what form it takes, how it is professed or how sincere it appears when it is given. The essence of love is its constancy even in adverse conditions. Love that is withheld for the failure to please is not very deeply rooted. Neither party discusses this fact, neither the controller nor the controlled, although the person being controlled suspects the love is false and fears discovering he is unlovable.

The price of a love is too high if it means that to preserve it you must mortgage your self-esteem or self-respect. A love that seeks to keep you from being you is not love at all, no matter what the other person insists.

The real problem in breaking away from controlling binds is that the person who has been controlled almost always is guarding a reservoir of anger that makes him feel guilty and frightens him when it comes to the surface. No wonder the amount of anger seems greater than justifiable, since it has been held in so long and since the person toward whom the anger is directed is often someone the controlled person has been led to believe he should love.

You can't control your feelings for the sake of anyone else. To do so is to sacrifice your mental health for the comfort of another person. What kind of a person would want you to injure yourself in that way? Do they really love you? Are they worth a self-sacrifice they would never repay?

When love is conditional it is not love at all.

12

Risks of Esteem

A risk of esteem fails when a person refuses to try his best, pretending that he does not care or that the risk is not suited to him.

A risk of esteem fails because a person does not risk as himself but acts in competition with others, out of anger or self-destructively out of guilt.

Risks of esteem are always anxiety provoking, for more than any other risk they seek to answer the question, "Am I good enough at what is most important to me?" And that alone is enough to stop many people in their tracks.

A RISK OF ESTEEM THAT FAILED

Martin found it difficult to please his parents because he did not know how to please himself. Father was a prominent businessman, who often extended himself beyond his means and so created an atmosphere of uncertainty in the household.

Martin was told that his responsibility was to perform in school and set a good example for his younger brothers and sisters, but he was constantly ridiculed by his father for "not having what it takes to make it."

Martin was too torn to rebel openly. He wanted to show his father that he was wrong, but when he brought home a report card with A's and B's his father commented only on the B's. When he brought home the A's, his father said that he had taken only four subjects. When he took additional subjects, his father told him he was one-sided because he had no extracurricular interests.

Martin decided to give up trying in school and to get involved in the sport he loved most: skiing. In a brief time he became an excellent skier and raced for his prep school. His father continued to ridicule him, saying he was wasting his time.

Martin pretended to ignore the complaints, although they touched a negative chord within him, a belief that he was really not good and might not make it. Afraid to trust others, he carried around feelings of self-doubt, and thought that they were unique to him.

Martin could not risk any pursuit in which his father had an interest. He dreaded competing with his father because being aggressive reminded him of being angry.

As a skier, however, where he challenged only the mountain, Martin became known for his reckless abandon, and was often kept out of competition by the coach in an attempt to teach him discipline. Disappointed, Martin quit the ski team and applied to and was accepted by his father's alma mater, Dartmouth, where skiing and being the son of an alumnus still carried some weight.

It also carried an enormous burden for Martin since many professors remembered his father as being a hard-driving, tough student. Martin was compared to his father by everyone who knew him, and the result was always disappointment.

Understandably, Martin found it difficult to apply himself in college, and took a leave of absence after the first year to find himself. The year was spent back-packing through the West, meeting people, trying out drugs and new life styles without really getting involved. He returned to college for two years, did barely passing work and left for another leave of absence during which he became involved with the meditation movement, studied astrology and the occult and for a time lived with a medium, twenty years older, whose only demands were sexual.

Martin's father took an extremely dim view of all this and was quick to say so. Martin would reply that his father would do well to take up meditation and learn to see the world in a different way; it would lower his blood pressure. Father would respond that he would pay for one more year of school, and after that Martin would be on his own.

When the son realized he had to earn his own living, he decided to finish college and apply to graduate school. The idea of graduate school sounded much better than working, but Martin never reached his old academic level. He felt as if he was holding something in reserve. He would frequently omit to study one part of the assigned work, or would forget to answer part of an exam, or would be late in handing in an assignment. He had an excuse for everything he did, explaining why his work was not his best, why he should not be judged by his performance. He claimed he could do much better, although no one ever saw the better work.

"I could get all A's if I studied hard," he told his father, "but I get C's and B's without doing much work."

Martin's father did not look kindly on these excuses and would call his son a "faker," to which Martin would respond that the father was trapped in the work ethic. After graduation Martin was on his own. Somehow he got into graduate school in psychology, but he left after the first semester because he felt the work was irrelevant to what he had learned about himself through meditation.

Martin took a position as an aide on the adolescent ward of a state hospital, where for the first time he seemed to like his work and to function well. He was able to get children to try harder at sports and to take some minimal risks. When his efforts came to the attention of the director of the ward, Martin was asked to set up a sports therapy program. Although he was well suited for this venture, the risk of acting in his own interests, taking responsibility and putting his talents on the line made him hesitate. The director insisted that he enlarge the program immediately. Martin agreed reluctantly. However, over the next two months he began to make the same kinds of unreasonable demands on the children that his own father had made on him. The program was discontinued when it became clear that Martin was bent on failing.

Out of work, educated but unskilled, he drifted from one job to another. He became sexually involved with every woman he could as a way of bolstering his falling self-esteem.

Feeling compassion for his son, Martin's father invited him into his business. Martin exchanged his knapsack for a new suit and joined the firm. It was a mistake from the very first day. His father found fault with his dress, demeanor, speech, attitude, thinking and mental capacity. All of the criticisms were taken quietly by Martin, who realized that this sad opportunity might be his last chance to make good. But the abuses he swallowed only made his self-image fall further. "If I were a man," he said to himself finally, "I would stand up to my father in front of everyone in the office and tell the s.o.b. off, but I can't even do that."

He left the family firm and returned to live near the Dartmouth campus, pretending to himself that somehow he was still involved with the college. He took a position as a ski instructor teaching children. He felt comfortable doing that, for there was little risk involved. He roamed the ski slopes during his off-hours, putting on a show for pretty lady beginners, impressing them with his ability.

But Martin could not take an important risk involving his self-esteem. He had been inhibited from trying hard when he was younger since his best efforts were not good enough to win praise. As he got older he found it increasingly difficult to feel secure taking any kind of risk, and would undermine his efforts rather than carry the work through to completion. He was not willing to reveal any part of himself that was not good, and he felt that little of him was worth anything.

Martin had a long road ahead before he would be able to risk. He needed to function below capacity merely to prove to himself that he could do something successfully. He would still have years of tentative growth before he could risk doing his best and being judged by his acts.

It is difficult for a person who has grown up without feeling loved to risk his self-esteem because to fail proves that he is unlovable.

Many people whose lives are one continual failure after another are really punishing themselves as a way of getting even with others. They feel guilty about being angry at someone for not loving them. It seems a circuitous and fruitless route to take in comparison with accepting reality and moving on. A risk of esteem is not a failure if it offers you a chance to test your ideas about yourself, to stretch your muscles, try your talents and see what you are worth, and to grow to the next step. Each person determines what he makes of his experience, but you can't find yourself unless you risk failing.

There is nothing so difficult as putting your best on the line, except perhaps to yearn for successes that never happened because you were too afraid to risk.

A risk of esteem is successful when you put yourself on the line, do your best and accept your performance as an honest reflection of yourself. There will always be some part of your performance that is not perfect. You will always make some mistakes, no matter how extensive your preparations.

A successful risk of esteem makes you more willing to risk the next time because you have overcome your hesitation to be yourself. When you try your best each succeeding risk can borrow some momentum from the risks taken before. When risks of esteem are successful your best self emerges. Your goals become clearer. You live your life simply by being you.

If you do not give your best when you take risks of esteem, the effort you reserve will spoil your performance and the next risk will be still more difficult to take.

A RISK OF ESTEEM THAT SUCCEEDED

Karen's life seemed to be filled with risks of one kind or another from the very beginning. She always seemed to be struggling to become something that her family never could understand. Something that she would have to seek by herself, unsupported and without guidance.

When Karen was born they had no expectations for her. They assumed that she would go to high school, find a job, meet some young man, marry and have children.

Karen gave her family nothing but problems.

When she was ten she insisted on playing the piano and

had dreams of becoming a performer someday. Unfortunately, the teacher Karen's parents reluctantly found for her taught her popular chords, quietly undermining her desire to learn classical technique.

Karen quit the piano dissatisfied with her progress, but still believing that there was something special within her and that all she needed was the opportunity to prove it. Her schoolwork had been excellent, but it began to deteriorate in the closing years of high school. She could no longer understand much of the class discussions. Because she was afraid of appearing stupid she told no one about her problem in comprehension.

Karen was slowly growing deaf but didn't know it. She tried harder without seeking help but her grades continued to decline. She assumed the problem was her intellect. Although she became head cheerleader to win admiration, no amount of superficial adulation could make her believe she was worthy. She wanted desperately to be different from her parents, to make something of herself, but sadly she did not seem to be making any progress. Her days in school became dreary and painful as each word she could not decipher seemed to point out her inadequacy.

In her senior year Karen met a boy who put on a very good act as the school intellectual. Everyone thought Ted was bright. In fact he was intelligent, but the display he made of his knowledge was obnoxious and the depth of his understanding was shallow. He was opinionated without being informed and put down anything he did not understand. He did all this with an arrogant air that took her in. She felt so insecure about herself that she assumed anyone who could act as confident as Ted must know what he was talking about. Ted showed an interest in Karen and she used this as proof that she was also bright.

It was a short-lived feeling.

At seventeen Karen discovered she was pregnant. She graduated from high school in her fifth month, married to Ted. Her secret plans for college that her parents never shared had been dashed to the ground, as were her hopes for becoming something better.

Karen had such high hopes and deep disappointments that she had become an expert at pretending and concealing her feelings of sadness. She was going to be a mother and so she decided to make the best of it.

She moved in with her parents while Ted was in the service, away for months at a time. While she was alone Karen read extensively to amuse herself. She tried to believe she was happy and tried to stop yearning for a world that was bigger and better than the one she knew. Her parents offered her no cruel comparison between the life she was living and what she had once hoped for. It should have been easy to forget her old dreams, but from somewhere deep within a feeling of unrest stirred, filling her with an incompleteness that could drown out the sun. Something was missing in her life and, although she did not know what it was, it gave her no rest.

When her baby was born Karen decided she would be the perfect mother, giving, warm and present for the baby, even though she could not be present for herself. When Ted returned they found a small apartment and set up a home. That is, Karen set up a home. Ted was just not interested in her or the baby and wanted to be free. Karen saw him for what he was, a dropout who would never make anything of himself. Their marriage became a battleground. Ironically, she became pregnant again. She had to decide whether to try to make the marriage work out for the sake of her children or whether to seek another solution.

What could she do? She had no education or money;

she did have some friends, but most of them were poor themselves and unable to help. Karen's deafness had grown worse and her feelings of isolation increased. She reflected, *Am I going to spend the rest of my life living with a man who doesn't know me, love me and couldn't care? Can I make a home for my children without love? Will I ever be able to find out who I am and what I want? Will I live in the shadows always hoping for something better and never knowing for sure?*

What have I got to lose? If I stay with Ted, I know I will never be anything. He doesn't care for me. I have to take care of myself. I have no job, no future, nothing. I have to be the one to take charge of my life. Even though I've pretended to be happy and other people will be shocked, I have to live my life for me.

Karen never planned how she would leave. If she did she probably would never have gone. One rainy afternoon during the summer, when she was six months' pregnant and staying at Ted's parents' summer cottage, she suddenly decided to go. She packed a suitcase, took her four-year-old daughter by the hand and got on a bus.

Karen decided to risk everything. She felt she could go no lower than living with Ted. The care of her children would have to be her responsibility. Admitting and shouldering that burden at least gave her a feeling of being in control of her own destiny.

She arrived in Boston with ten dollars in her pocketbook and took a small apartment in a tenement. The next day she went to the welfare office seeking financial assistance.

She convinced a social worker to find aid for her education. She applied to college and nursing school and was accepted. Karen began a demanding schedule the next fall. Each day she left her children at a child care center, commuted to school and came home at night to play with them, studying into the early morning hours. She knew that if she failed her life would be terrible, and that she would never be able to face herself. No matter how bad she felt, or how tired, she kept thinking of her goal and of saving herself. Her life was in her own hands and she knew it.

During this time Karen began to date men again and found that she was both attractive and intelligent. Each new discovery about herself led her to risk more. She graduated from college and nursing school with honors at the same time and went into graduate nursing. Eventually she became a nursing practitioner, and shared a private practice with a pediatrician.

In spite of all this, Karen saw her new career only as a step, but a step to what? She was not sure, but she had learned something positive about herself that she did not know before and had a strong wish to share it with other women who might be caught in the same trap as she.

The old fear of not being good enough never really left Karen. The more she accomplished, the more aware she became of her old fears. When she discovered she was deaf and had a reason for not understanding, she found it easier to ask others to repeat their remarks. A real handicap sometimes takes the pressure off, allowing a person to work harder without fearing failure so much. There were still times when she found it easier to hide behind a role or to pretend that she really didn't care when she really did. This became harder to do, but in time Karen began to take her losses and her successes with equal honesty.

At this writing, Karen's career is still developing. She continues to face new challenges and to test her new strengths. She lectured widely to adolescent and high school groups and organized programs for teenagers in turmoil. She trained as a therapist and began to treat adults as well as children. Rather than pretend that she had been happy all of her life, she grew comfortable with the pain she had experienced and used it as a guide to help understand others.

Where once she had been so afraid of taking any risk involving her self-esteem, Karen now dealt with the world exclusively by putting her worth, her opinions and her judgment on the line. There are many ways of measuring success, but where esteem is concerned, success is the ability to be whatever you are without pretending to be something else. Karen was no longer pretending to be happy, to be a good daughter or a wife making the best of it. She was willing to use her own life as an example to help others, to share her vulnerabilities rather than conceal them and to take a stand for herself and face whatever life offered without hiding.

A risk of esteem offers an answer to the question: Am I good at the thing I want to be good at? You can easily get cold feet in the middle of a risk like that. It is common to pretend or to avoid trying hard to protect your self-image.

A risk can be more closely planned than was Karen's, but the actual act of taking it seems overwhelming and terrifying in each case. It is the singer standing on the stage waiting for the curtain to go up. It is the batter at the plate, and the fighter in the ring. All risks of esteem have at their core the moment of truth. The arena changes. The crowd and the need to please vary. But victory, even when applauded, is always silent, always private and unsharable, and even in the moment of success a little sad, a little let down from the ideal.

The applause is not as important as taking the risk. Merely stepping onstage is succeeding; the rest is performance either good or bad. The victory is accepting the best role you can play and using your discomfort as a guide to plan the next risk, understanding the part you play in your own story.

Karen did not know she would make it. If you climbed into her mind before she acted, you would discover that she was only aware of one step at a time even though she had a distant goal of being better. She knew only what she had to do at each step. She gave everything she could when it counted. She acted in the present, knowing, "This is it!"

Because Karen accepted the responsibility for shaping her life, she grew. Whether she succeeds in becoming what she wants is not as important as her knowing that she is the one taking her own risks, the one who will fail or win.

Her life is finally her own, and at last she is free.

A BETTER LIFE

Taking a risk of your esteem is the beginning of becoming free. Your dream of a better life is your creation. There may not be a model you can look to and follow. You have to make it yourself. It is your idea, your thought. It becomes real when it is shared or when it is put into action, when it becomes your way of life.

If we are brave we grow into an image of our highest self, giving up pretenses and striving to become what we suspect we could be if we tried a little harder. The final push is a lonely act for no one can know or understand what you are becoming but yourself. The reassurance you get from others is often as insincere as their criticism and does not mean much. When it comes to esteem each person must decide to risk or not on his own. There is no shared glory although the people who love you will feel joy for you and the people who are afraid to try will find reasons why your achievement wasn't all that great. You can't win with everyone.

In some ways your achievement will always fall short. This should not be seen as a loss, but as a statement of hope for improvement and as a reason for continuing to excel. When we succeed, our sense of accomplishment and completion gives us a new perspective of where we have been, and at that moment we glimpse what lies ahead. Each achievement opens the way to the next step.

As we grow we discover the process never stops. If we take the right risk, giving our best effort, the next risk will feel more comfortable because we gain the confidence of our own success. The next work for an artist is always harder than the one before. And with each new risk the issues of "Can I do it?" and "Am I good enough?" become at least partly resolved. We are concerned with how to take the next risk and doing our best, but as we get better our standards grow too.

Growth is always a risk. It is like leaping out of an airplane and parachuting into a clearer, more honest reality, becoming whole, real, your best.

The vision you see for your world and your life is yours alone. You owe it to yourself to find your dream and make it happen for you. The worth of your efforts to you is not that they are great, but that they are yours, that *you* tried, that *you* gave your life a meaning from which you could take strength, making you feel whole. There is no other strength worth leaning on in life. All of the creations of man's genius emanate from this point, each man taking his inner dream and making this vision real by risking to give it form.

When it comes to risking our self-esteem, we are all artists and our life is our creative work.

13

The Dos and Don'ts of Risking

DO HAVE A GOAL

A risk taken without a clear purpose is in trouble from the start. It is hard to tell when you have lost and should conserve your resources. It is just as hard to tell when you have won and should consolidate your gains.

DO KNOW THE LOSS INVOLVED

If you don't expect the loss, it will catch you by surprise and undermine your efforts. If you don't expect the loss, you don't understand the risk. Don't add confusion to an already complicated situation.

DO ACT DECISIVELY

Once you have decided the risk is worthy of you and the time is right, you should act. You've considered the negative, weighed it all before. So focus on the factors you can affect and make them work for you.

DON'T IGNORE PROBLEMS

Problems will not ignore you. You will find each other eventually. Make the meeting be as much on your terms as possible. You'll be in a better position to shape the outcome.

DON'T PRETEND YOU'RE SURE WHEN YOU'RE FRIGHTENED

Your fear is your guide to safety. Ignoring it is like ignoring a fire alarm. If the fear won't go away, maybe you're still in danger or risking too much.

DON'T BE UNREALISTIC

No one gets rescued by supernatural forces these days. You'll have to save yourself in the tight places. Consider what is the best effort you are capable of making. Don't plan on being able to deliver more than that. Don't plan on reserves you don't already control.

DO ASK QUESTIONS

It's your life and you have to know as much as possible. If you are going to take a risk unnecessarily, you are most likely going to do so because you were afraid to ask questions. It's better to appear stupid than to make a big mistake.

DON'T COUNT ON BEING ONE HUNDRED PERCENT SUCCESSFUL

No one ever is, and you'll only be unnecessarily disappointed. Your self-confidence will drop and you won't have as much energy to invest next time. If you succeed at a modest goal you are better off than failing at a big risk. Bravery counts only when you win. When you lose, bravery is just being foolish.

DON'T MISPLACE YOUR EMOTIONS

Don't risk out of fear, anger, hurt, guilt or depression. These feelings should be resolved on their own, not through a risky act. Emotional risks should be taken only with emotional issues. If you are angry you should risk expressing the anger, but you should not risk driving a hundred miles an hour because you feel angry with your boss. Don't act out your feelings, in other words. They will mess up your risks.

DO TAKE TIME TO CORRECT MISTAKES

Even when the act of risking is under way mistakes can be fixed. A good risk can be made better by compensating for the errors you discover.

DO BE BRAVE

This takes enormous courage. The reason you feel afraid is not because you are weak, but because you are real. The brave people are those who act in spite of fear, not those who have none. Fools are the only ones who do not fear danger.

DO KNOW YOUR LIMITS

Know when you would never act. Know when you would act without question. Know what you would compromise in terms of safety. If you are looking for a totally safe risk you are only fooling yourself. Know your limits, define the conditions under which you would take a reasonable risk.

DON'T RUSH

Take enough time to know what you are doing. Prepare beforehand. If possible, practice your risk in private. Go through it in your mind if you can't go through it in fact. Imagine yourself there. What would you do? What would you say? How would you react? Merely setting your mind working in the right direction is often all you need to become familiar with what you fear.

DON'T DELAY

Commit yourself to the risk before you take it. Don't look into the chasm to see how deep it is. It's the width you must jump and that's most important. It will always seem deeper when you go looking for excuses not to commit. Delaying at the moment of leaping is dangerous. Hesitation is not in the interests of safety, unless something totally unpredicted goes wrong. Then the risk is off till you reassess the situation.

DO GIVE OTHER PEOPLE CREDIT FOR HELPING YOU

You'll make allies out of people who want to help you. You need all the friends you can get when you risk, and the best friends are those who have already given. Return the gift with thanks. Friends who feel slighted can do you more damage than enemies.

DO YOUR BEST

Don't just try. Trying is a tentative commitment. It means, "I'll see if I can do it." You intend to *do it* when you risk. If you don't intend to succeed, you intend to fail.

DON'T ARGUE WITH REALITY

Some mountains you can leap, some you can't. What sounds like great encouragement for the troops may make for memorable last words. Your goal is to succeed and enjoy the results.Try to remember that.

DO MAKE A TIMETABLE

This doesn't mean you have to follow it if everything goes wrong, but a good schedule can be a strongly persuasive force because it gives direction and reinforces the belief that your plan is working. Anything that aids your ability to predict makes risking easier. So does knowing the next step.

DON'T COMBINE RISKS UNNECESSARILY

Many risks have several outcomes, to begin with. To try to take more than one risk at a time compounds the loss and therefore the anxiety. It undermines your ability to recoup, because a failure at one will take away the confidence you need to succeed at the other.

DO MAKE A PLAN, BUT DON'T STICK TO IT LIKE A RELIGION—IT MAY BE WRONG

You are responsible for everything in your life, including changing plans. Just because you make a plan doesn't mean that it's right or that all the factors were properly considered.

DON'T CHANGE HORSES IN MIDSTREAM

If your plan is a good one, it should allow you to expect and accept the negative results of your risk without panicking over them, so don't run at the first sign of blood. Risking, like surgery, involves cutting away some good to get rid of a lot of bad.

DON'T RISK JUST TO PROVE YOURSELF

This is hazardous risking. You get away with it a few times if you are lucky and grow up in time. A lot of the time you don't have the chance to grow up.

DON'T BLAME OTHERS FOR YOUR FAILURES

It's always your fault.

DON'T GIVE UP TOO SOON

It is not going to be easy like one-two-three—so have patience and perseverance.

DON'T HOLD ON FOREVER

You can tell when something is lost. If the loss is overwhelming and you have no choice, hanging on might be better than letting go, but this risk is one that should not have been taken in the first place. Let a bad situation end. Don't prolong it.

DON'T RISK YOUR LIFE UNLESS THE ODDS OF DEATH ARE CERTAIN

If the doctors give you two years to live without the operation, but claim that in a year you will be too weak to survive, you'd better consider having it now. You risk when the odds are best.

DO TRY TO UNDERSTAND HOW THE ODDS FLUCTUATE

Know the factors that influence your risk. Use the odds in your favor. When conditions are changing, observe them as long as you can without giving too much away. Sailing when the tide is full may be only an approximation, but it works best.

DON'T TRUST BLINDLY

Thieves and con men will try to take advantage of your inhibitions and work on your blind spots. Know your own base qualities: your greed, your self-centeredness, your dishonesties. Then no one can play to them and lead you by the nose. You have to be your own master when you risk.

DO LIST EVERYTHING THAT CAN GO WRONG—AND WHY

You'll pick up problems sooner because you'll be looking for them.

DO LIST EVERYTHING THAT SHOULD GO RIGHT—AND WHY

What items in these two lists are likely to change? Which are likely to remain assets? Liabilities? Can an asset turn against you? Can you use a liability to your advantage?

DO TAKE YOUR OWN RISKS

Whenever you allow someone to take your risks for you, you are putting your fate into the hands of someone who cannot take your interests to heart the way you would. If you need someone to take your risks, you are gaining no experience and when the day comes that you will have to risk on your own, you are more likely to be overwhelmed, more likely to fail.

DON'T TAKE ANYONE ELSE'S RISKS

If you take someone's risks for them, they do not have the opportunity to grow. When you take a child's risks for him, you are acting as protector. To act as another adult's protector implies possession, invites resentment and is sticking your nose in other people's business. If you take another person's risk and fail, you deserve all the trouble you'll get.

DO BE SERIOUS

Risking makes everyone anxious and anxiety makes people joke and pretend a situation isn't serious when it is. Don't be fooled into playing around when the stakes are high. This may be a tension breaker, but it could lead you to be careless and self-destructive.

DON'T TAKE TIME OUT WHEN YOU ARE RISKING

The time of risking is the moment of truth. You'll have to spend all of your time focused on the risk at hand.

You'll be working overtime without breaks, without thanks, till the crisis is past. When you are risking, you are risking, and nothing else is important. Of course when a risk is long term you can take breaks, but all time spent risking should be spent in earnest concentration. The secret of success in most risks is not letting up while there is something you can do to affect the outcome in a positive way or to limit losses.

Do leave well enough alone

If you have your desired result, if the pendulum has swung in your direction, you have momentum going. Keep the pressure on, but don't overdo it. There is sometimes very little difference between a nice head of steam and a runaway process.

Epilogue

Because you are unique and your life situation is totally different from anyone else's, there is no pat answer to your problems. This book has attempted to show you how to analyze the changing variables involved in taking a risk, and how to focus on the key issues upon which success and failure hang.

There is no substitute for motivation. Nothing fortifies a person as much as knowing he has honestly faced the painful potential losses in his struggle and is prepared to do battle in spite of them. It is not easy. Even the best prepared plans, the most clear cut road, can suddenly turn rough and you can lose the day.

The risks you take depend on your vision for yourself. If you go through life with no ideal, it is unlikely that anything you risk will bring you lasting joy. The risks worth taking are those that lead you to create the best life possible for yourself. The happiest life is one where you feel comfortable being yourself, without apologizing for the way you are or pretending to be something you are not.

If there is any hope for any of us it is that we should be happiest living our lives as our best selves, not in competition with others but in realization of our potential. The risks we must take to attain a more honest, freer life are always more difficult at the beginning, when the dishonesty we must concede in ourselves is greatest and the fear of discovering what we are really like is most inhibiting. As we risk more on the road to finding our potential, the risks become easier to take and the goals we seek begin to become part of our daily experience. The life we create for ourselves becomes our reality and our world becomes limitless.

Somewhere behind every risk should be a life worth risking for.

DALE CARNEGIE—THE MAN WHO HAS HELPED MILLIONS TO GREATER ACHIEVEMENT—CAN HELP YOU!

Start enjoying your job, your personal relationships—every aspect of your life—more fully with these classic books. Check the ones you want and use the coupon below to order.

____ 54435-7 HOW TO DEVELOP SELF-CONFIDENCE AND INFLUENCE PEOPLE BY PUBLIC SPEAKING $3.95

____ 49269-1 HOW TO ENJOY YOUR LIFE AND YOUR JOB $2.95

____ 62394-X HOW TO STOP WORRYING AND START LIVING $4.50

____ 60197-0 THE QUICK AND EASY WAY TO EFFECTIVE SPEAKING $3.95

____ 61699-4 HOW TO WIN FRIENDS AND INFLUENCE PEOPLE $4.50